W9-AWY-576

PLANETARY SCIENCE
RESOURCES

IMAGES, DATA, AND READINGS

DEVELOPED AT LAWRENCE HALL OF SCIENCE, UNIVERSITY OF CALIFORNIA AT BERKELEY
PUBLISHED AND DISTRIBUTED BY DELTA EDUCATION

FOSS Middle School Curriculum Development Team
Dr. Lawrence F. Lowery, Principal Investigator
Linda De Lucchi, Co-Director
Larry Malone, Co-Director
Sue Jagoda, Curriculum Developer
Anthony Cody, Curriculum Developer
Dr. Susan Brady, Curriculum Developer
Dr. Kathy Long, Assessment Coordinator
Cheryl Webb, Program Assistant
Carol Sevilla, Graphic Designer
Rose Craig, Artist
Mark Warren, Equipment Manager

Planetary Science Multimedia Design Team
Dr. Marco Molinaro, Director
Dr. Susan Ketchner, Project Manager
Leigh Anne McConnaughey, Principal Illustrator
Wolf Read, Senior Illustrator
Sue Whitmore, Graphic Artist
Richard Blair, Head Programmer
Tom McTavish, Head Programmer
Terence Wong, Assistant Programmer
Aaron Walburg, Assistant Programmer
Alicia Nieves, Quality Assurance
Guillaume Brasseur, Computer Administrator and QA Manager

Special Contributors and Consultants
Dr. Andrew Fraknoi, Astronomer/Consultant; Marshall Montgomery, Materials Design
Dr. Jan Woerner, Visiting Professor, Earth Science Education; Alan Gould, Astronomy Education Consultant
Dr. Cary Sneider, Astronomy Education Consultant; Ted Stoeckley, Teacher; Dr. Terry Shaw, Teacher
Rockman ET AL., Evaluators

Delta Education FOSS Middle School Team
Mathew Bacon, Jeanette Wall, Bonnie Piotrowski, Tom Guetling, Dave Vissoe, Grant Gardner,
John Prescott, Joann Hoy, Cathrine Monson

National Trial Teachers
Victoria Milani, Booth-Fickett Magnet School, Tucson, AZ; Evelyn Rayford, North Heights Junior High School, Texarkana, AR
Pris Brutlag, Parsons Middle School, Redding, CA; Judith Hartman, Eliot Middle School, Altadena, CA
Suzi Owen, Westside Charter School, Rio Linda, CA; Lorraine Usher, Borel Middle School, San Mateo, CA
Carol LeCrone, Mt. Garfield Middle School, Clifton, CO; Bill Daly, Northglenn Middle School, Northglenn, CO
Kana Estrada, Northglenn Middle School, Northglenn, CO; Sheree Vessels, Southern Oaks Middle School, Port St. Lucie, FL
Lisa Evans, Southern Oaks Middle School, Port St. Lucie, FL; Linda Rose, Derby Middle School, Derby, KS
Jeffrey Schroeder, Pine Island Public School, Pine Island, MN; John Kuzma, McManus Middle School, Linden, NJ
Gayle Dunlap, Walter T. Bergen Middle School, Bloomingdale, NJ; Donna Moran, Walter T. Bergen Middle School, Bloomingdale, NJ
Teri Dannenberg, Memorial Preparatory School, Garland, TX; Linda Silvas, Holmes Middle School, Alexandria, VA
Roed Freeland, Salk Middle School, Spokane, WA; Scott Stier, Badger Middle School, West Bend, WI
Doug Zarling, Badger Middle School, West Bend, WI

Lawrence Hall of Science

FOSS for Middle School Project
Lawrence Hall of Science, University of California
Berkeley, CA 94720 510-642-8941

...because children learn by doing.®

Delta Education
P.O. Box 3000 80 Northwest Blvd.
Nashua, NH 03063 1-800-258-1302

The FOSS Middle School Program was developed in part with the support of the National Science Foundation Grant ESI 9553600. However, any opinions, findings, conclusions, statements, and recommendations expressed herein are those of the authors and do not necessarily reflect the views of the NSF.

Copyright © 2001 by The Regents of the University of California
All rights reserved. Any part of this work (other than duplication masters) may not be reproduced or transmitted in any form or by any means, electronic or mechanical, including photocopying and recording, or by an information storage or retrieval system without permission of the University of California. For permission, write to Lawrence Hall of Science, University of California, Berkeley, CA 94720.

542-1382
1-58356-402-0

Planetary Science Resources
Table of Contents

IMAGES FOR PLANETARY SCIENCE *p. 1*

DATA FOR PLANETARY SCIENCE *p. 33*

READINGS ON PLANETARY SCIENCE *p. 45*

FOSS Planetary Science Resources

IMAGES

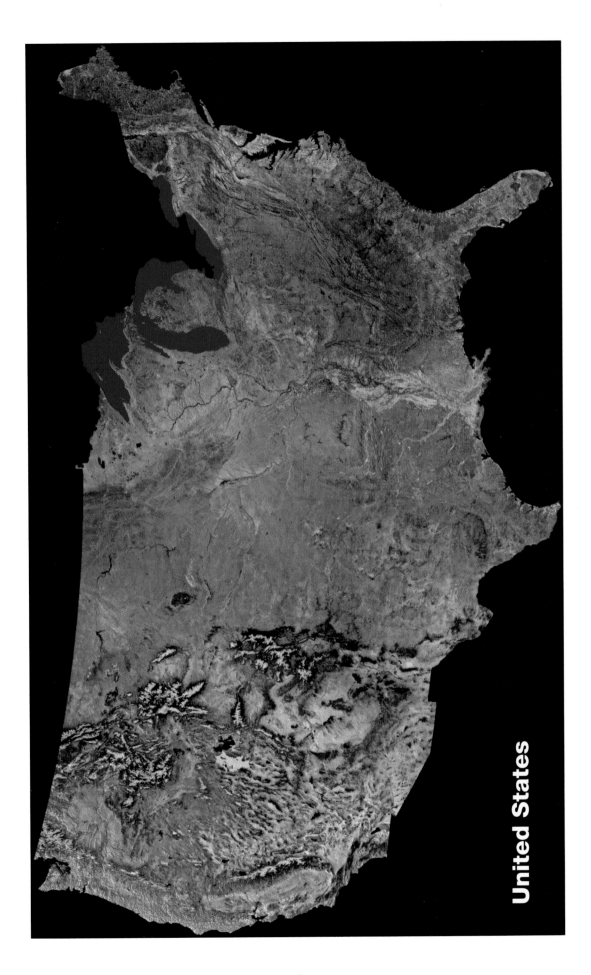

United States

Bret Harte Neighborhood

Bret Harte Community

6359-81 WILD 15/4 UAGA-4 Nr.13114 152.81 07-06-93

San Francisco Bay Area

Southwest Region

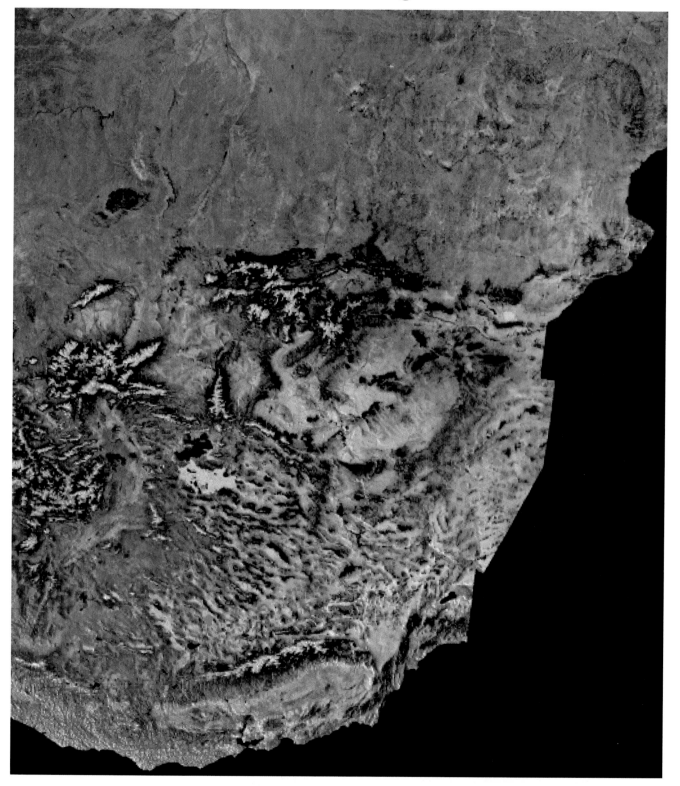

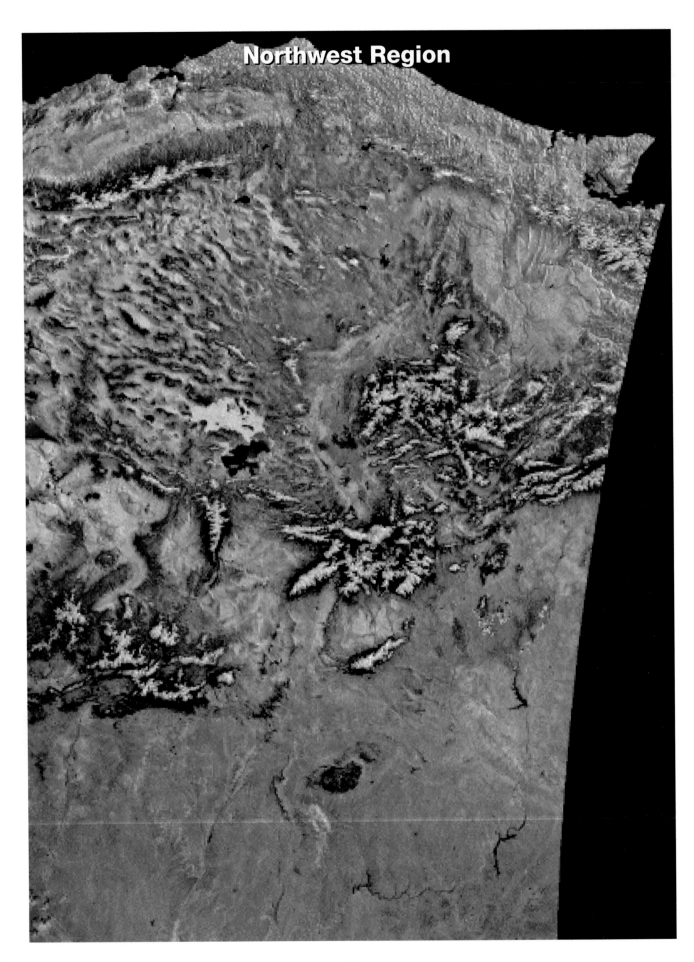

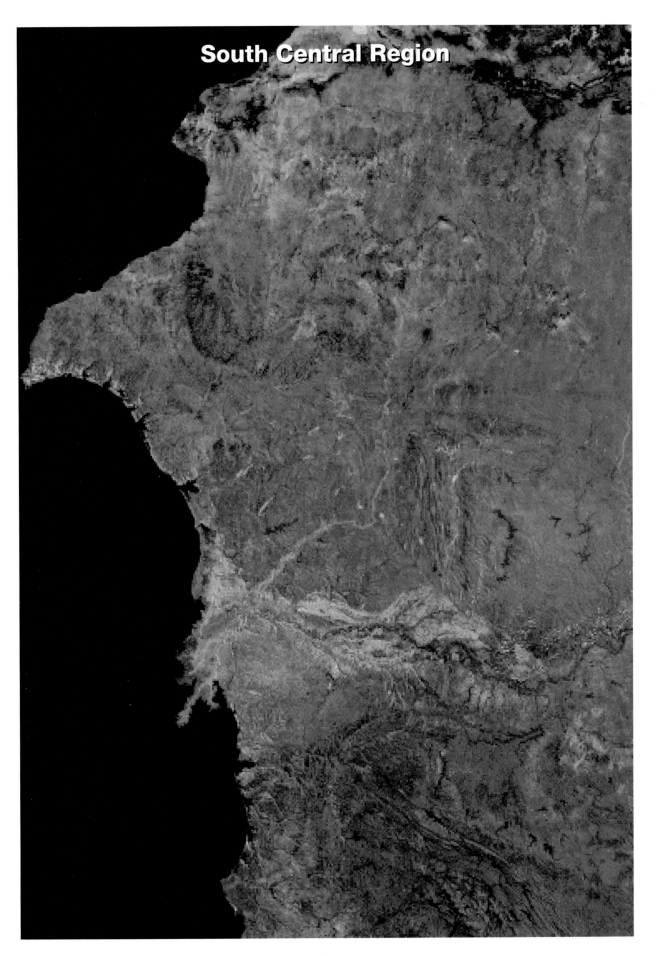

South Central Region

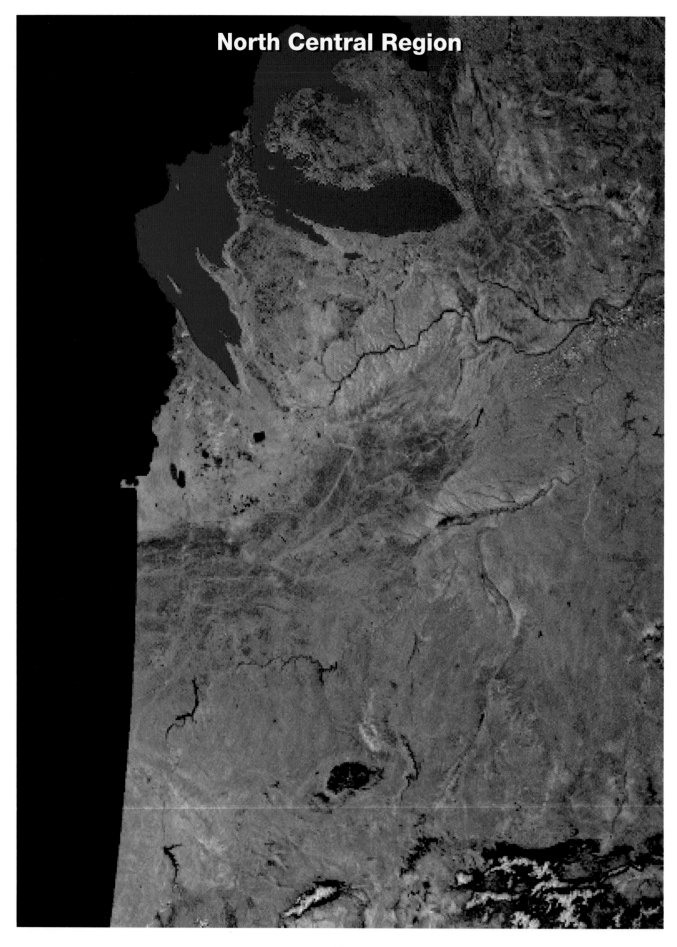

Southeast Region

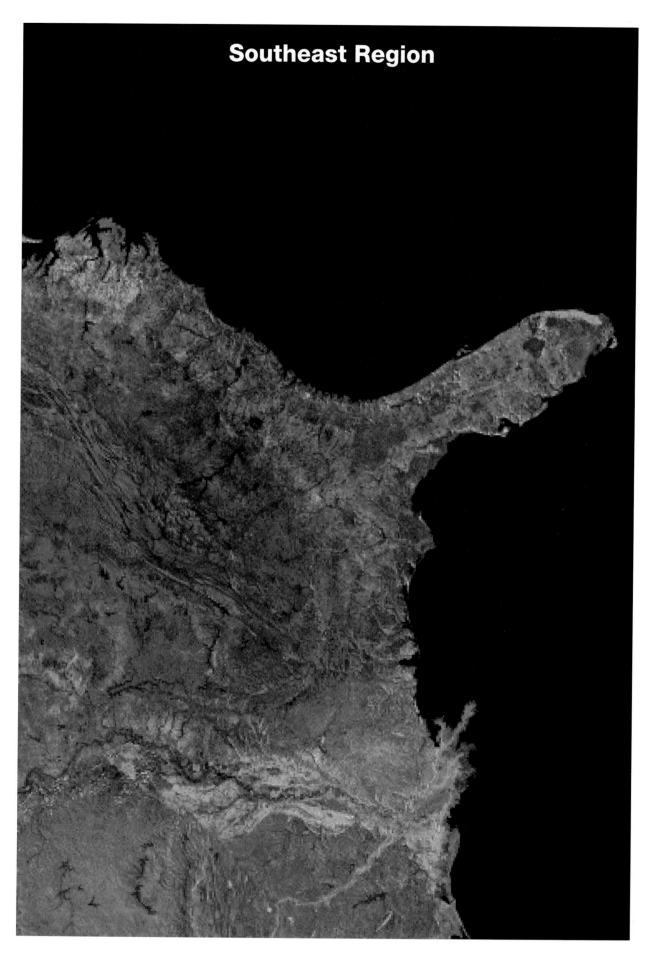

North America

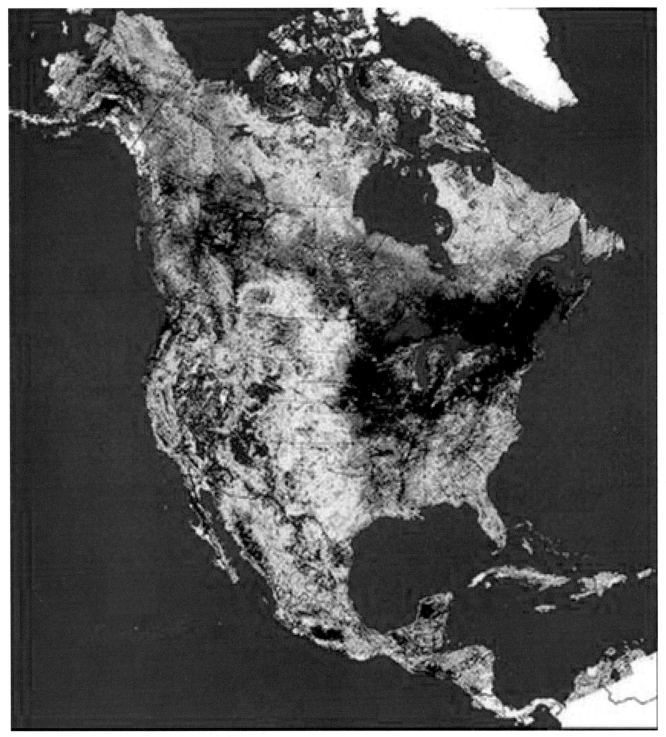

Planet Earth

Washington, DC

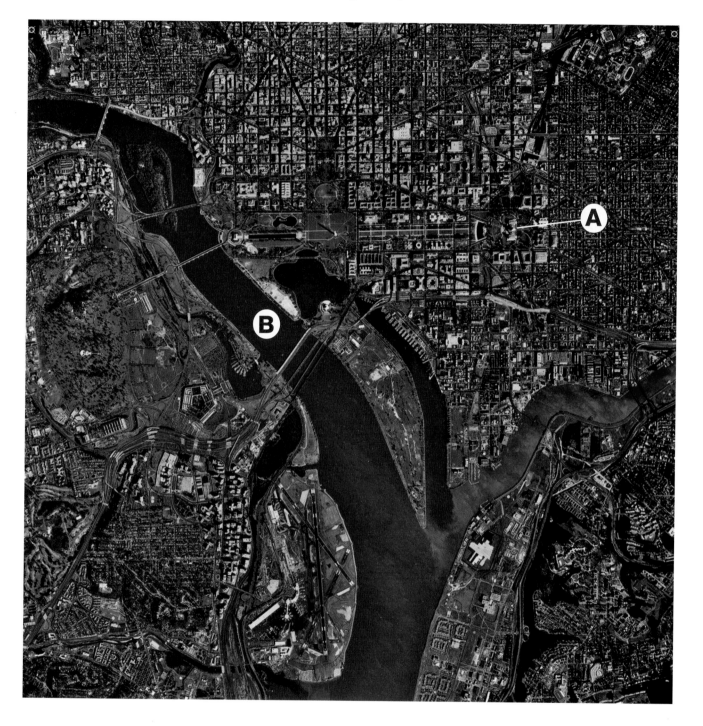

Full Moon

Moon Photo

Archimedes

Aristillus

Lunar Alps

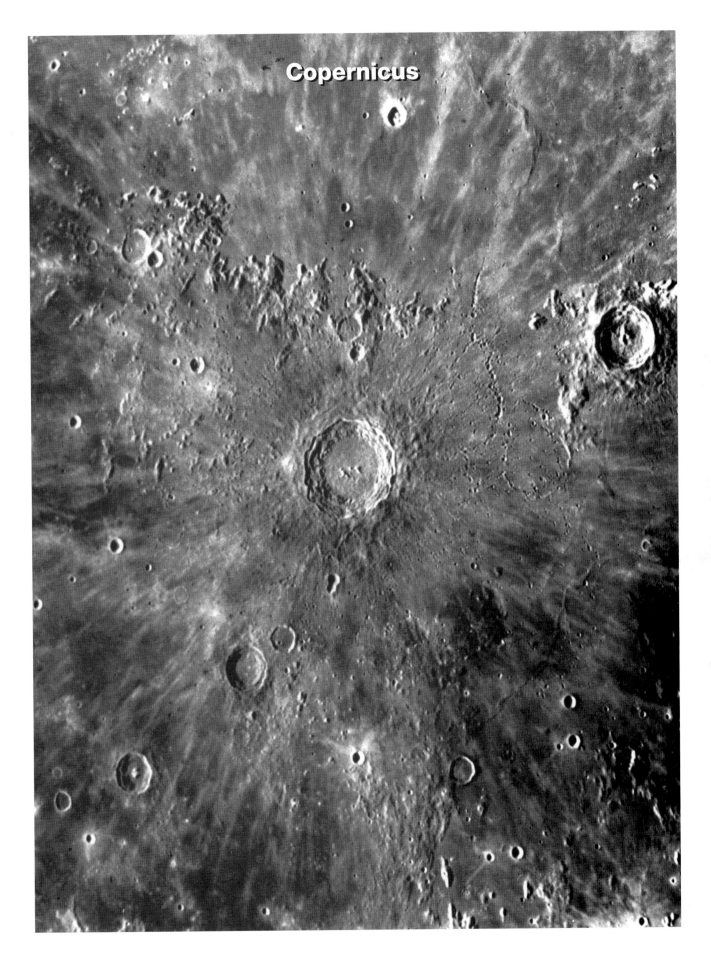

Copernicus

Sea of Serenity

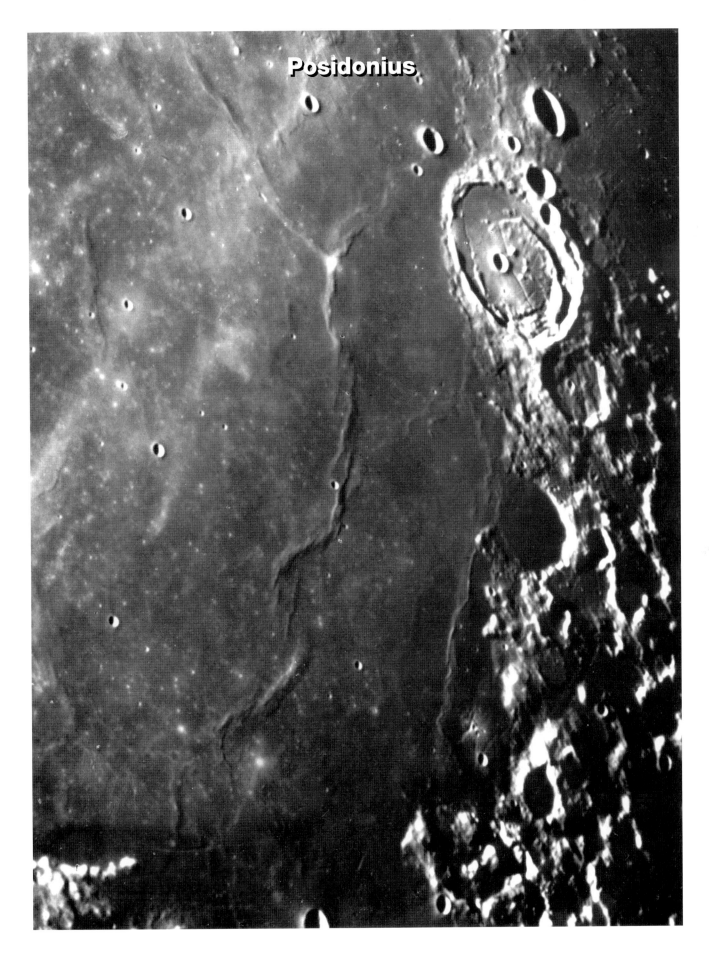

Posidonius

Stofler

Tycho and Clavius

Face of the Moon

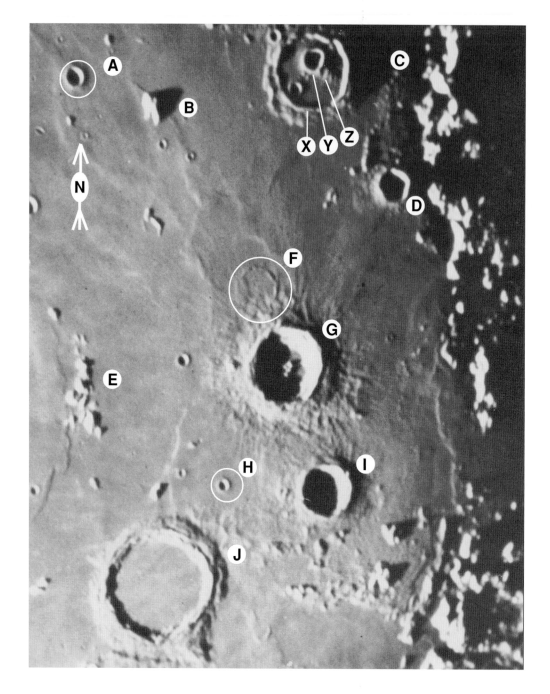

Barringer Crater, Arizona

Gosses Bluff, Australia

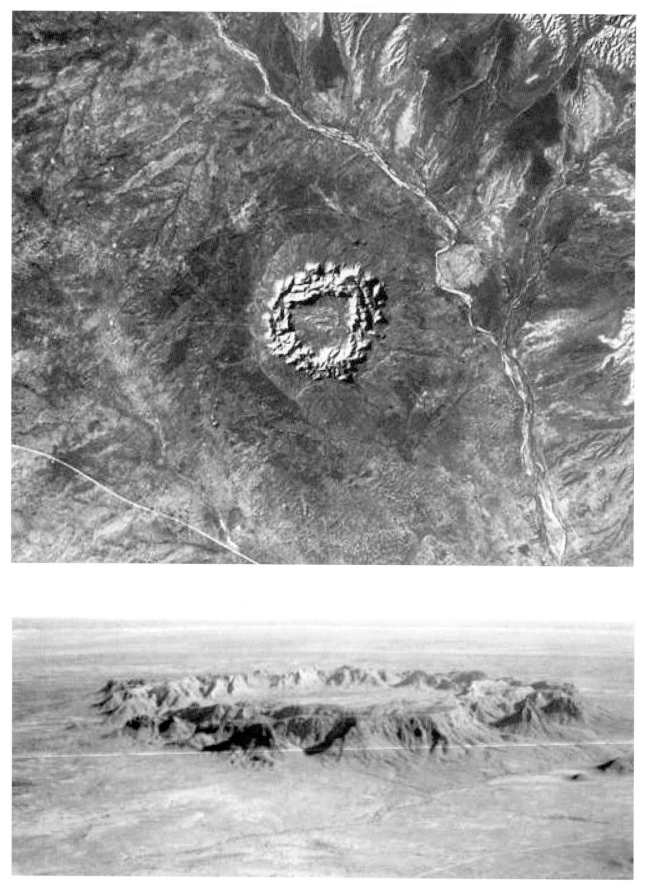

Manicouagan Crater, Canada

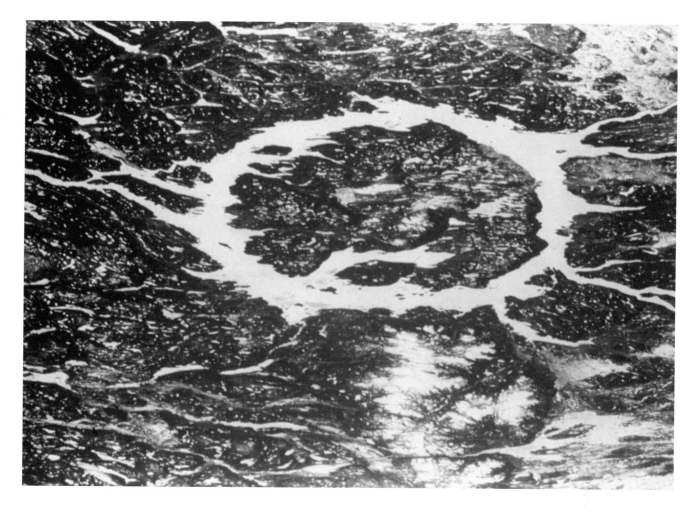

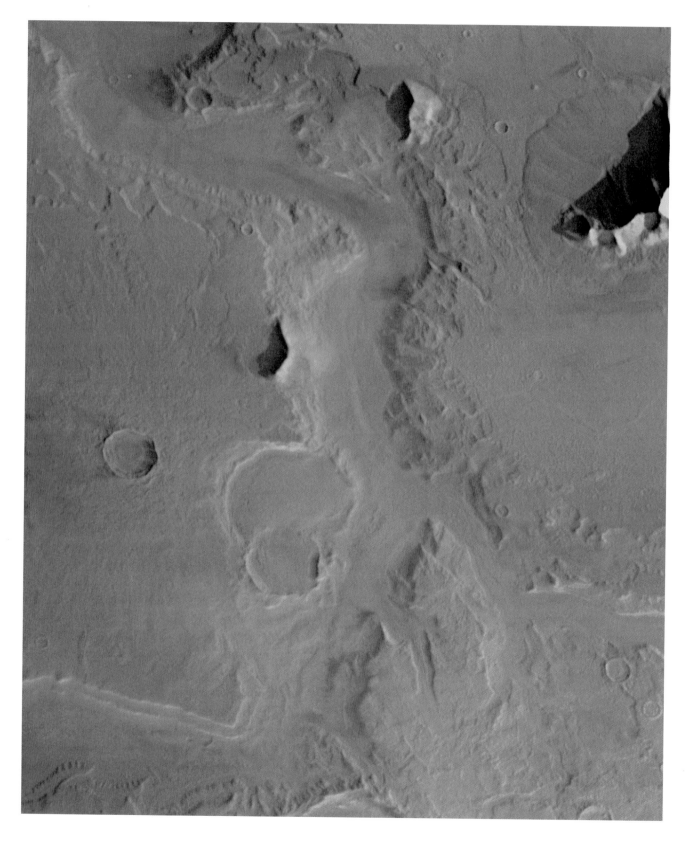

Phases of the Moon Sequence Puzzle

Starting with the full Moon, write the letters associated with the images to show the sequence of the phases of the Moon.

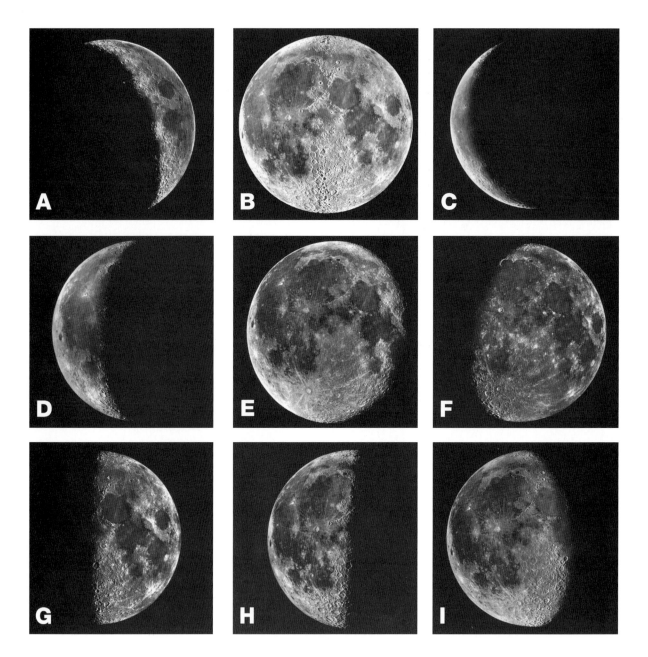

FOSS Planetary Science Resources

DATA

Sun, Planets, and Satellites by Size

Name   Name of planet or satellite   **Radius**   Radius of planet or satellite (in km)
Orbits   Sun or planet it orbits   **Density**   Grams per cubic centimeter
Distance Distance to the Sun or to   **Orb. Period** Orbital period (in Earth days)
            the planet (in 1000 km)   **Rot. Period** Rotational period (in Earth days)

Name	Orbits	Distance	Radius	Density	Orb. period	Rot. period
Sun			695,000	1.41		25–36
Jupiter	Sun	778,330	71,492	1.33	4333	0.4
Saturn	Sun	1,429,400	60,268	0.69	10,760	0.4
Uranus	Sun	2,870,990	25,559	1.29	30,685	−0.7
Neptune	Sun	4,501,200	24,764	1.64	60,190	0.7
Earth	Sun	149,600	6,378	5.515	365	1
Venus	Sun	108,200	6,052	5.25	225	−243
Mars	Sun	227,940	3,397	3.94	687	1
Ganymede	Jupiter	1,070	2,631	1.94	7	7
Titan	Saturn	1,222	2,575	1.88	16	16
Mercury	Sun	57,910	2,440	5.42	88	59
Callisto	Jupiter	1,883	2,400	1.86	16.7	17
Io	Jupiter	422	1,815	3.55	1.8	1.8
Moon	Earth	384	1,737	3.34	27.3	27
Europa	Jupiter	671	1,569	3.01	3.6	3.6
Triton	Neptune	355	1,350	2.07	−5.9	−5.9
Pluto	Sun	5,913,520	1,160	2.05	90,800	−6.4
Titania	Uranus	436	789	1.70	8.7	8.7
Rhea	Saturn	527	765	1.33	4.5	4.5
Oberon	Uranus	583	775	1.64	13.5	13.4
Iapetus	Saturn	3,561	730	1.21	79	79
Charon	Pluto	20	635	1.83	6	6
Umbriel	Uranus	266	585	1.52	4	4
Ariel	Uranus	191	579	1.56	2.5	2.5
Dione	Saturn	377	560	1.43	2.7	2.7
Tethys	Saturn	295	530	1.21	1.9	1.9
Enceladus	Saturn	238	250	1.24	1.4	1.4
Miranda	Uranus	130	236	1.15	1.4	1.4
Mimas	Saturn	186	196	1.17	1	1
Janus	Saturn	151	98 × 96	0.67	0.7	0.7
Epimetheus	Saturn	151	72 × 54	0.7	0.7	0.7
Phobos	Mars	9	14 × 10	2.0	0.3	0.3
Deimos	Mars	23	8 × 6	1.7	1.3	1.3

Time Zones of the Lower 48 States

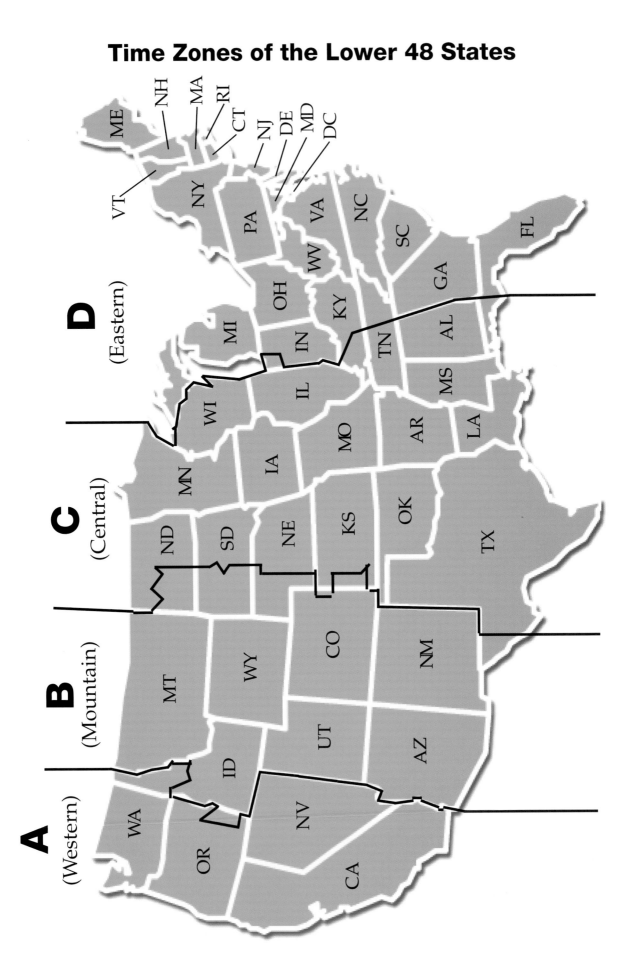

A (Western)

B (Mountain)

C (Central)

D (Eastern)

World Time-Zone Map

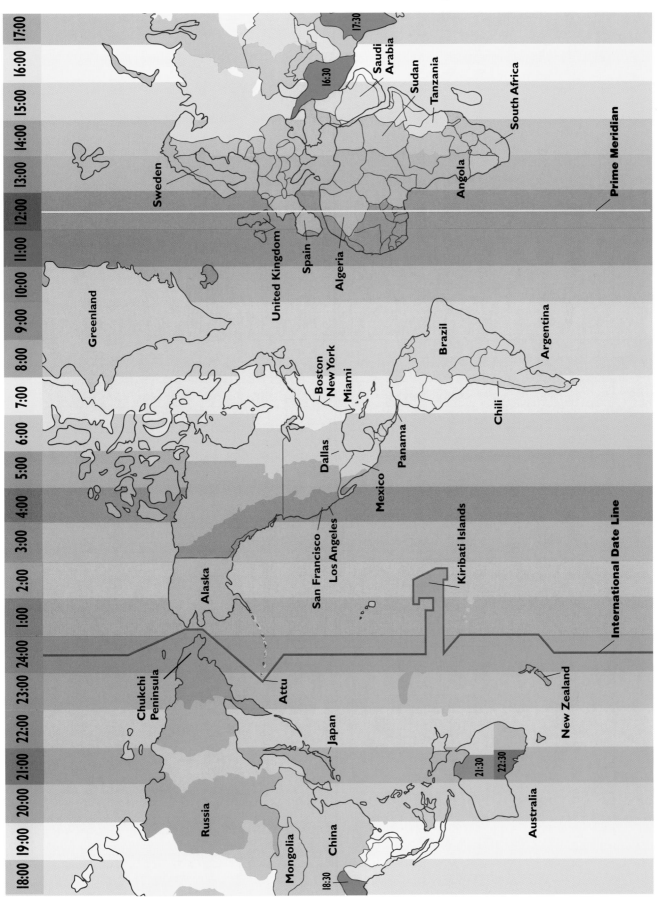

Moonrise/Sunrise Data

Here are the moonrise and sunrise times for June 1996.

Date	Moonrise	Sunrise	Moon Phase
June 1	8:29 p.m.	6:35 a.m.	full Moon
2	9:31 p.m.	6:34 a.m.	
3	10:30 p.m.	6:34 a.m.	
4	11:23 p.m.	6:34 a.m.	
5		6:34 a.m.	
6	12:11 a.m.	6:34 a.m.	
7	12:56 a.m.	6:34 a.m.	
8	1:37 a.m.	6:34 a.m.	third quarter
9	2:16 a.m.	6:34 a.m.	
10	2:54 a.m.	6:34 a.m.	
11	3:33 a.m.	6:34 a.m.	
12	4:13 a.m.	6:34 a.m.	
13	4:55 a.m.	6:34 a.m.	
14	5:38 a.m.	6:34 a.m.	
15	6:25 a.m.	6:34 a.m.	
16	7:13 a.m.	6:34 a.m.	new Moon
17	8:03 a.m.	6:34 a.m.	
18	8:54 a.m.	6:34 a.m.	
19	9:45 a.m.	6:34 a.m.	
20	10:37 a.m.	6:34 a.m.	
21	11:28 a.m.	6:35 a.m.	
22	12:21 p.m.	6:35 a.m.	
23	1:14 p.m.	6:35 a.m.	
24	2:08 p.m.	6:35 a.m.	first quarter
25	3:05 p.m.	6:36 a.m.	
26	4:04 p.m.	6:36 a.m.	
27	5:06 p.m.	6:36 a.m.	
28	6:09 p.m.	6:37 a.m.	
29	7:12 p.m.	6:37 a.m.	
30	8:13 p.m.	6:38 a.m.	
July 1	9:11 p.m.	6:38 a.m.	full Moon

Earth/Moon Comparison

Moon with Landing Sites

Mission	Launch date	Location of landing	Mission objective
Luna 9	January 31, 1966	Ocean of Storms	Photographic exploration
Luna 13	December 21, 1966	Ocean of Storms	Ground study
•*Apollo 11*	July 16, 1969	Sea of Tranquility	First manned mission
•*Apollo 12*	November 14, 1969	Ocean of Storms	Second manned mission
Luna 17	November 10, 1970	Sea of Rains	Lunokhod 1 vehicle
•*Apollo 14*	January 31, 1971	Fra Mauro Highlands	Third manned mission
•*Apollo 15*	July 26, 1971	Apennine Mountains	Fourth manned mission
•*Luna 20*	February 14, 1972	Sea of Fertility	Sample collection
•*Apollo 16*	April 16, 1972	Region of Descartes	Fifth manned mission
•*Apollo 17*	December 7, 1972	Taurus-Littrow region	Sixth manned mission
Luna 21	January 8, 1973	Sea of Serenity	Lunokhod 2 vehicle
•*Luna 24*	August 9, 1976	Sea of Crises	Sample collecting

•Missions for which rock samples are included in the kit.

Moon Rock and Mineral Key

Sample	Name	Important Properties	High-lands	Mare
	Pyroxene	Dark gray/green mineral. Opaque. Luster: glassy. Cleavage: breaks into pieces with flat, shiny surfaces. May fracture in splinters.		
	Ilmenite	Black to brownish-black mineral. Heavy. Opaque. Luster: metallic to submetallic. Magnetic.		
	Feldspar (plagioclase)	White to gray mineral. Translucent. Luster: metallic to submetallic. Cleavage: breaks into pieces with flat, shiny surfaces.		
	Olivine	Green mineral. Composed of rounded, sandlike grains. Luster: glassy.		
	Anorthosite	Purplish gray rock composed mostly of feldspar. Pieces of feldspar can be easily identified if the texture is coarse.		
	Basalt (fine-grained)	Fine-grained, dark-gray igneous rock without noticeable luster. Without holes.		
	Basalt (vesicular)	Fine-grained, dark-gray to black igneous rock containing many holes or cavities that once contained gas bubbles.		
	Breccia	Rock composed of fragments of other rocks melted together. Multicolored.		
	Glass	Rounded, often beadlike rock particles, usually orange. Transparent to translucent. Astronauts called it "orange soil."		
	Norite	Dark-gray to black igneous rock with small shiny surfaces.		

Moon Rock Formation

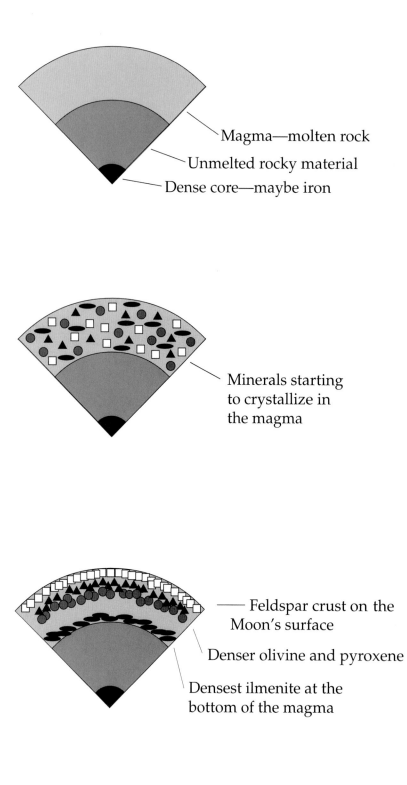

Magma—molten rock

Unmelted rocky material

Dense core—maybe iron

Very early in the Moon's history it was covered in a magma ocean of unknown depth, but certainly pretty deep—some think more than 500 km.

Minerals starting to crystallize in the magma

As the magma ocean cooled, the minerals in the magma began to crystallize into clumps of

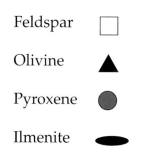

Feldspar ☐

Olivine ▲

Pyroxene ●

Ilmenite ⬭

Feldspar crust on the Moon's surface

Denser olivine and pyroxene

Densest ilmenite at the bottom of the magma

The densest mineral, ilmenite, sank in the liquid magma; olivine and pyroxene didn't sink as far; and the least-dense feldspar floated to the surface, where it formed the light-colored crust of the Moon.

U.S. Planetary Missions, 1962–2013 and Beyond

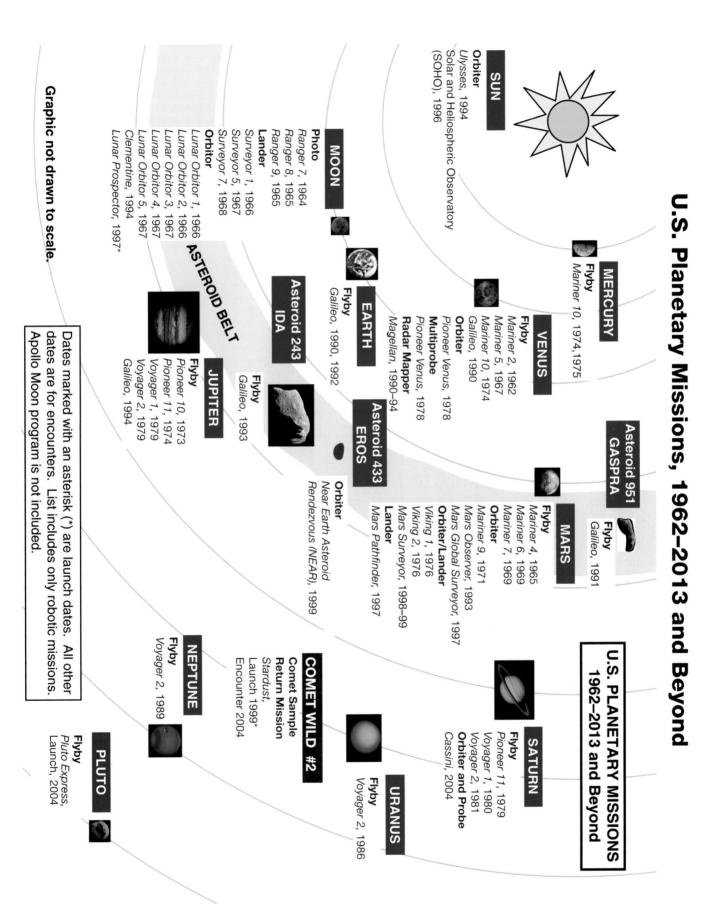

SUN

Orbiter
Ulysses, 1994
Solar and Heliospheric Observatory
(SOHO), 1996

MOON

Photo
Ranger 7, 1964
Ranger 8, 1965
Ranger 9, 1965
Lander
Surveyor 1, 1966
Surveyor 5, 1967
Surveyor 7, 1968
Orbiter
Lunar Orbiter 1, 1966
Lunar Orbiter 2, 1966
Lunar Orbiter 3, 1967
Lunar Orbiter 4, 1967
Lunar Orbiter 5, 1967
Clementine, 1994
Lunar Prospector, 1997*

MERCURY

Flyby
Mariner 10, 1974, 1975

VENUS

Flyby
Mariner 2, 1962
Mariner 5, 1967
Mariner 10, 1974
Galileo, 1990
Orbiter
Pioneer Venus, 1978
Multiprobe
Pioneer Venus, 1978
Radar Mapper
Magellan, 1990–94

EARTH

Flyby
Galileo, 1990, 1992

ASTEROID BELT

Asteroid 243 IDA

Flyby
Galileo, 1993

Asteroid 433 EROS

Orbiter
Near Earth Asteroid
Rendezvous (NEAR), 1999

JUPITER

Flyby
Pioneer 10, 1973
Pioneer 11, 1974
Voyager 1, 1979
Voyager 2, 1979
Galileo, 1994

Asteroid 951 GASPRA

Flyby
Galileo, 1991

MARS

Flyby
Mariner 4, 1965
Mariner 6, 1969
Mariner 7, 1969
Orbiter
Mariner 9, 1971
Mars Observer, 1993
Mars Global Surveyor, 1997
Orbiter/Lander
Viking 1, 1976
Viking 2, 1976
Mars Surveyor, 1998–99
Lander
Mars Pathfinder, 1997

SATURN

Flyby
Pioneer 11, 1979
Voyager 1, 1980
Voyager 2, 1981
Orbiter and Probe
Cassini, 2004

COMET WILD #2

Comet Sample
Return Mission
Stardust,
Launch 1999*
Encounter 2004

NEPTUNE

Flyby
Voyager 2, 1989

URANUS

Flyby
Voyager 2, 1986

PLUTO

Flyby
Pluto Express,
Launch, 2004

U.S. PLANETARY MISSIONS
1962–2013 and Beyond

U.S. PLANETARY MISSIONS
1962–2013 and Beyond

Graphic not drawn to scale.

Dates marked with an asterisk (*) are launch dates. All other
dates are for encounters. List includes only robotic missions.
Apollo Moon program is not included.

FOSS Planetary Science Resources
READINGS

The Accidental Discovery of America: The First Voyage of Columbus

Before the time of Columbus, European traders made long and perilous overland journeys over thousands of miles to get to the Far East—China, India, Persia, Japan, and Southeast Asia. Europeans called this whole region the Indies—land of many riches. Some of the prizes they sought were spices, gold, and silk. The cost of bringing silk and spices from the Indies to Europe was high, because of the difficult overland journey.

Columbus figured that, if he could find a sea route to the Indies, he could reduce the time and expense of overland transportation, and thus sell his goods at a much greater profit. He could become the richest merchant of all!

In Columbus's time, the world known to the Europeans did not include the Americas. They had no idea that North America, South America, Central America, or any of the Caribbean islands existed. They thought that there was only one ocean, the great Ocean Sea, which extended west an undetermined distance.

In 1488, the Portuguese captain Bartholomeu Dias made a voyage in which he sailed down the west coast of Africa, around the southern tip (the Cape of Good Hope), and up its eastern coast to the Indies. This became known as the eastern route to the Indies.

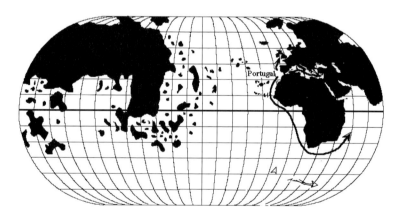

Eastern route to the Indies

But Columbus had another plan. He wanted to sail *west* across the Ocean Sea to reach the Indies from the other side.

When Columbus sought funds from King Ferdinand and Queen Isabella of Spain, they listened. They sent him to Spain's best university to talk with professors to determine if his plan was practical.

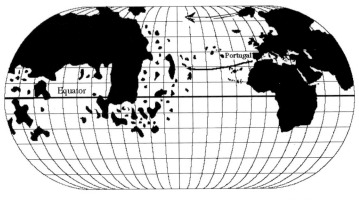

Columbus's proposed route to the Indies

Many people incorrectly believe that Columbus wanted to prove that Earth is round. But Columbus already knew it is round. He had studied the various forms of scientific evidence, and he had seen islands appear to rise from the ocean as he sailed toward them. On a flat Earth, this would not happen.

Columbus tried to convince the kings and queens of England, France, and Spain to finance his journey, but failed many times. His plan was considered risky because it called for sailing west into unfamiliar waters rather than following the long but relatively safe eastern route.

In those days, all educated Europeans knew that the world is round. Columbus didn't need to prove it. Scholars had known this for over 1800 years. So what did Columbus argue about with the professors? It was not about the *shape* of Earth, it was about *how big* Earth is.

Columbus thought Earth is only about 18,000 miles (30,000 km) around. The trip from Europe to the far Indies using the trusty, but long, eastern route was 12,000 miles. So, reasoned Columbus, the Ocean Sea could be no more than 6000 miles—probably less.

The professors, on the other hand, argued that Earth was about 24,000 miles around, making the Ocean Sea 12,000 miles or more across, a distance that would require about 3 months to cross.

The world according to Columbus

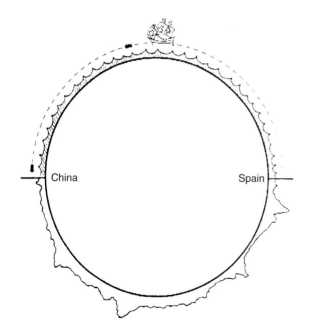

And that was the problem—the ships of that time could store only enough food and water for a trip of about 1 month. The scholars argued that Columbus and his crew would die of thirst or starvation.

The world according to the professors

Columbus was taking a big risk to sail across the Ocean Sea, and King Ferdinand and Queen Isabella were taking a big risk by investing money from the Spanish treasury.

Finally it was agreed. In 1492, Columbus set sail in his three tiny boats, the Niña, the Pinta, and the Santa Maria, from southern Spain, which is about 36° north latitude. He sailed south to the Canary Islands at about 28°, and then straight across the great Ocean Sea until he arrived at an island that he thought was in the Indies.

Columbus believed that the islands he explored were part of the Indies. But, as it was determined, after voyages of Amerigo Vespucci, Columbus had landed not in the East Indies, but in the "New World." The island, in fact, was one of the Bahamas, just off the southern tip of

Florida! Columbus was lucky that those islands happened to be there. If he had not struck land when he did, he and his crew would have died of thirst, as the scholars had warned.

So who did discover America? Columbus discovered the Americas, but by accident. He was headed for Asia, but ran smack into a whole continent that he was totally unaware of. However, there is evidence that the Viking explorer Bjarni

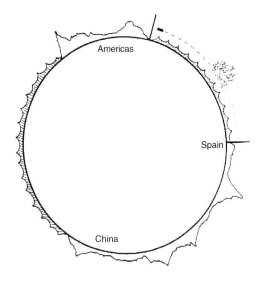

Modern view of the world

Herjolfsson visited North America in the summer of 986, followed soon after by Leif Ericsson. Over 1500 years ago, the Chinese Buddhist priest Hwui Shan sailed to the Americas across the Pacific Ocean, calling his discovery Fusang, meaning "fabulous." And there is archaeological evidence suggesting that around 2800 years ago African sea-roving traders may have sailed to present-day southeastern Mexico.

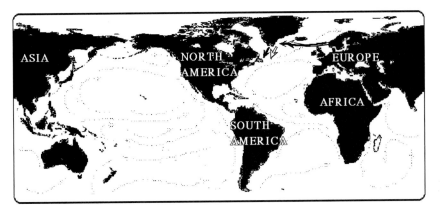

Viking route

Think Questions

When Columbus arrived in the Caribbean, people were living on the islands he "discovered." So who did discover America? Was it Columbus? Or did he simply follow in the footsteps of earlier adventurers? What do you think?

Columbus sailed down to the Canary Islands, at 28° north latitude, just off the coast of north Africa, and then headed west. Eventually he ran into America, pretty much on the 28th parallel. How do you think Columbus was able to cross the ocean without wandering north or south by accident?

Illustrations in this article first appeared in *Who "Discovered" America?* from the Planetarium Activities for Student Success (PASS) Project, volume 10, Lawrence Hall of Science, University of California, Berkeley, CA 1992.

Eratosthenes:
The First Person to Measure Earth

During the third century B.C.E., more than 2000 years ago, the Greek librarian and mathematician Eratosthenes heard a story that interested him. It was said that in the city of Syene on the Nile River, at noon one day out of the year, June 21, the Sun shone directly down an abandoned well, illuminating the dry bottom. This simple observation started Eratosthenes thinking. For that to be true, he reasoned, the Sun would have to be directly over the well. And if the Sun were directly overhead, a pole, standing perfectly straight up and down right next to the well, wouldn't have any shadow at all!

Eratosthenes had reason to believe that the Sun was very far from Earth, so any beam of light striking Earth would be virtually parallel to every other beam of light reaching Earth. Therefore, if the Earth were flat, the Sun would be directly overhead *everywhere* at the time it was directly over the dry well. Furthermore, poles placed absolutely vertically in the ground anywhere on Earth would cast no shadow at that time.

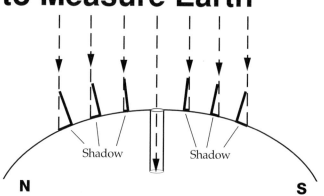

Eratosthenes discovered that poles outside the city of Syene *did* cast shadows, and the farther north they were, the longer the shadow. For Eratosthenes this provided evidence of a round Earth.

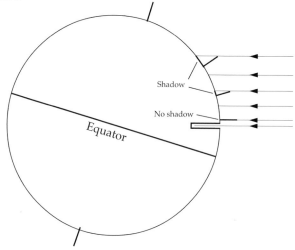

But he was not done. Suppose that Eratosthenes and a friend arranged to observe the shadows cast by identical poles, placed in different locations, at the same exact time (noon) on June 21. In Syene, next to the well, no shadow was observed. The Sun's rays were perfectly parallel to the pole. But in Alexandria, 800 km to the north, there was a shadow. Eratosthenes reasoned that the pole in Alexandria had to be at a different angle than the incoming rays of light from the Sun. Because both poles were perfectly straight up and down, the surface of the land must also be at a different angle—like on a curved surface!

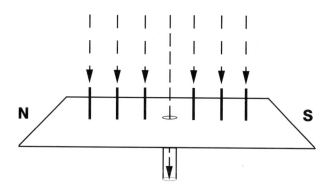

On the other hand, Eratosthenes reasoned, if Earth were round, poles placed straight up and down in the ground would be shadowless only in a very small area; everywhere else poles would have shadows.

After measuring the shadow in Alexandria, Eratosthenes used a protractor and geometry to determine that the Sun shone on the city of Alexandria at an angle of 7.2°. Remember that number—it's important.

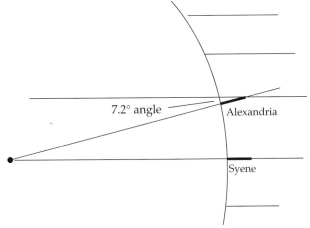

Eratosthenes also knew that distance around an arc (circle) can be described in degrees. A complete circle is 360°. A little simple math tells us that 180° describes one-half of a circle, and 90° describes one-quarter of a circle.

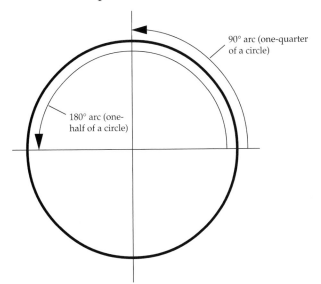

Eratosthenes wanted to know what part of a circle 7.2° represented. Using the same reasoning, he divided 360° by 7.2° and got 50. Now he knew that 7.2° is 1/50 of a circle.

Eratosthenes then measured the distance from Syene to Alexandria in a standard unit of the time, the stadium. He found that it was 5000 stadia between the two cities. So 5000 stadia was

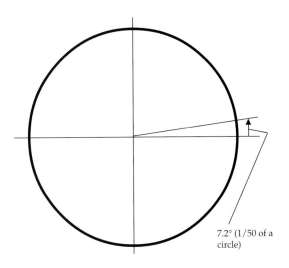

1/50 of the distance around the circle that represented the circumference of Earth. He then multiplied 5000 by 50, because he knew that the distance between the two cities was 1/50 of the distance around the world. He found that our planet is 250,000 stadia in circumference.

Simple and elegant science and math; monumental thinking. Because no one today knows for sure how long a stadium was, it is difficult to argue with the result Eratosthenes calculated. Modern scholars, using a plausible value for the stadium of 185 m, come up with an estimate of 46,250 km. And that's pretty good when compared to today's accepted circumference of 40,074 km.

Now there is no question about the shape of Earth. We've all seen pictures taken from space, and it is round. But think for a moment about the accomplishment of Eratosthenes. He measured Earth with a shadow and a protractor more than 2000 years ago.

Think Question

Think about all the preparation and measuring Eratosthenes had to do to measure Earth. What do you think was the most difficult part of the project?

Father Moon

From Siriono people of eastern Bolivia.

Yasi had a son. One day the boy was playing with a jaguar and was accidentally killed. The jaguar was terrified and ran deep into the forest to hide forever. Yasi wanted to find out who the killer was, but none of the animals would tell him. This so enraged Yasi that he gave the howler monkey a long neck, put spines on the porcupine, and burdened the tortoise with a heavy shell.

Yasi was still furious, so he leaped up into the night sky to search for his son's killer. He searched all across the land and the sky. Each day Yasi got dirtier and dirtier until he was completely covered with soil and leaves. He stopped by a stream to rest and clean himself. Each day he rested, Yasi washed a little bit of his face. Finally he was completely rested and clean, and he resumed the search for his son's killer.

Yasi is still wandering the skies today, spending half his time hunting and half his time resting. When he returns from the hunt, his face is completely covered in dirt. He washes off a little of the dirt each day until his face shines brightly once again.

RONA IN THE MOON

One bright evening, Rona went to fetch water from the stream for her children. In her hand was a basket containing a calabash [a hollow, dry gourd] to hold the water. While on her way, the Moon suddenly disappeared behind a cloud, and the path being narrow, with projecting roots of trees and bushes, she kicked her foot against a root. In her momentary anger, she cursed the Moon, saying, "You cooked-headed Moon, not to come forth and shine!"

These words displeased the Moon, who came down to Earth and seized Rona. She caught hold of a ngaio-tree that was growing on the bank of the stream; but the Moon tore the tree up by the roots, and flew away, taking Rona, the tree, and the calabash in the basket far up into the sky. Her friends and children, thinking she was a long time away, went to look for her. Not finding any traces of her, they called, "Rona, O Rona, where are you?" She answered from the sky, "Here I am, mounting aloft with the Moon and stars."

When it is a clear night, especially when the Moon is full, Rona may be seen reclining against the rocks, her calabash at her side, and the ngaio-tree close by.

From Maori people of New Zealand.

From *Myths and Legends of the Polynesians* by Johannes C. Andersen, Dover Publications, Inc.

Moon and His Sister

The Moon was a good-spirited and friendly Indian whose face was even brighter than that of the Sun. Moon had one sister, a small star who was often seen beside him, and he had many other star friends.

One day Moon gathered all his friends together for a great potlatch. His house was very small, and soon the guests had taken up all the space.

As soon as Moon's sister arrived, Moon asked her to fetch water for him in several buckets. This was not an easy task, as it was winter. She had to deal with the cold, howling wind as she walked to get the water. The water was frozen by the river, and she had to chip through the ice to fill the buckets.

She walked back to the house with her heavy burden, only to find that there was no room inside for her. She called to her brother, "Where can I sit?"

Moon was in a very good mood, and he just grinned at his sister. "There isn't enough space for even a mouse in here. I guess you will have to sit on my shoulder," he laughed.

Moon's little sister was not in the mood for his good humor. She took him at his word and jumped onto his shoulder. There she sits even today, holding on to her water buckets. Moon is not as bright as he once was, as the shadow from her buckets dims his face.

Native Americans of the northwest coast of North America held large parties and feasts called potlatches. The host would provide great amounts of food and give extravagant gifts to the guests.

TALE OF THE RABBIT

There had been four Suns in previous ages, and all had ended in catastrophic destruction. The gods came together to create a new and final Sun. To create the Sun, one of the gods would have to jump into the fire, the hearth of the gods. The gods gathered at the hearth at midnight to determine which god would make the sacrifice and become the Sun.

Two gods volunteered. One of them was wealthy and strong, the arrogant Tacciztécatl, and the other was poor, sick, and frail, the god Nanahuatzin. Both agreed to die in order to raise the new Sun.

But when the strong god approached the fire, the flames flared high, and, frightened, he drew back from the edge. His fellow gods shouted encouragements to him to take the leap, but he could not.

Humble Nanahuatzin approached the fire, and, without hesitating, he leaped into the flames. His body sizzled, crackled, and burned. This gave Tacciztécatl the courage to jump, and he did. The other gods waited in the darkness for signs of the dawn and Nanahuatzin's transformation into the fifth Sun.

The gods kept arguing among themselves as to where the Sun would first appear. Each one took up a position looking in a different direction so they would be sure to see the Sun as it first came up. And finally the Sun appeared brilliant and red in the east, the direction of creation and new life. Following the Sun, Nanahuatzin, was a second very bright ball, Tacciztécatl, reincarnated as the Moon. Both balls remained still, and in order to get them to move across the sky, the rest of the gods had to sacrifice themselves in the fire.

But before they died, one of the gods did something to the Moon. He grabbed a rabbit and hurled it into the Moon's bright face, darkening it tremendously. You can still see the imprint of the rabbit on the face of the Moon today.

This is an Aztec story of a willing sacrifice on behalf of the world's renewal.

BAHLOO, *Moon Man*

Bahloo, the Moon, was lonely high up in the empty sky, so he decided to visit Earth. When the campfires were burning and the girls were dancing, Bahloo came down close to Earth and lowered his shining face to speak to the girls. They were frightened by this bright round white thing and ran away.

The next night he returned to find two other girls sitting on the riverbank. "How beautiful the moonlight is," sighed one of the girls. This was encouraging to Bahloo, and he decided to come closer to the girls. He broke into a run, puffing and blowing, his big belly shaking. The girls were surprised by Bahloo, and they didn't know whether to laugh or shout for help. They ran away a safe distance and stood there staring back at the Moon.

Bahloo's feelings were hurt, and he sat down by the riverbank and cried. The girls felt sorry for Bahloo and returned. They invited him to ride in their canoe to the other side of the river. But Bahloo was so big that, when he stepped into the canoe, it rocked and tipped, and then turned over, dumping Bahloo into the water. The round shining Moon sank down, down into the water and his light became dimmer and dimmer. The girls laughed and ran home.

Bahloo was very embarrassed. He climbed into the sky without anybody noticing and remained hidden for several days. Gradually, he regained his courage and grew round and bright for all to see. But when he remembered the girls and how they laughed at him, he began to get smaller and soon went out of sight. Every month, Bahloo grows round and bright and full of courage, and every month he remembers his fall into the river and shrinks away to hide.

Aboriginal tribal myth, Australia

The Controversy about Lunar Crater Formation

Moon Map

Narrator: In the 1960s two distinguished geologists thought about the craters on the surface of the Moon and came up with two different explanations for their origin. They studied photographs of the Moon's surface, similar structures on Earth, and, later, samples of Moon rocks returned by the *Apollo 11* mission. The evidence convinced Dr. Jack Green that most of the craters were volcanic in origin; Dr. Eugene Shoemaker was convinced that the craters were created when pieces of flying space debris, called meteoroids, slammed into the Moon's surface. We will now hear a presentation of the evidence by the two scientists. After the positions have been stated, we will think about how we might obtain additional information to support one position or the other.

Planetary Science Resources Book
pages 16–21

Green: I think most of the major features on the Moon are volcanic in origin, including the maria, the craters, and the mountains. I see most of the features arising from internal processes—eruptions and the movement of molten material—on a hot Moon. It is undoubtedly true that the Moon has been impacted by flying objects, as has Earth, but most of the craters are probably the result of volcanism.

CD-ROM
Moon binder/Geology/Landforms on the Moon
• *Alpine Valley*
• *Lunar Maria*

CD-ROM
Moon binder/Geology/Craters on the Moon
• *Moon Crater Locator Maps*
• *Eratosthenes Crater*

Shoemaker: I think most of the craters on the Moon were formed by impacts, that is, high-speed solid objects that slammed into the Moon's surface. Additional craters were probably caused by chunks of the Moon itself flying out as a result of large impacts. There seems little doubt that the Moon has had some volcanic activity and many of the rocks appear to be volcanic, but I think the Moon has been cold for a very long time. Most of the craters appear to have been made after the rock was in place.

Planetary Science Resources Book
page 21

Green: Copernicus Crater is one of the most prominent craters on the Moon. It is eight times wider than the Grand Canyon and twice as deep. It has a prominent group of mountains in the center. To me, Copernicus is a typical caldera, that is, a

CD-ROM

Moon binder/Geology/Craters on the Moon
- *Moon Crater Locator Maps*
- *Copernicus Crater*
- *Copernicus Crater (Apollo 12)*

Planetary Science Resources Book

page 27

CD-ROM

Earth binder/Geology/Craters on the Earth
- *Earth Crater Locator Map*
- *Barringer Crater*
- *Barringer Crater 2*
- *More about Barringer Crater*

Planetary Science Resources Book

page 21

CD-ROM

Moon binder/Geology/Craters on the Moon
- *Copernicus Crater Rays*
Moon binder/Geology/ Landforms on the Moon
- *Hadley Rille*

Planetary Science Resources Book

page 21

basin resulting from volcanic action. A caldera forms when a large volcanic area becomes less active. The center of the volcanic area contracts or collapses when the molten material retreats or drains away. It is a slow process that may take hundreds of thousands of years. During that time it is reasonable to expect some periodic volcanic activity that might create a group of mountains in the center of the caldera. We see craters of this kind on Earth, such as Crater Lake in Oregon.

Shoemaker: I have arrived at the conclusion that Moon craters are impact craters by studying impact craters here on Earth. One of the best examples of a recent impact crater here on Earth is Barringer Crater in Arizona. It is about a kilometer across. It formed around 50,000 years ago when a piece of matter about the size of a house slammed into what is now the desert east of Flagstaff.

The hole is large compared to the object that caused it, because of the amount of energy released at the moment of impact. The material that filled this crater at one time was thrown out in all directions, creating a raised rim, like a low hill, all around the edge of the crater. These two features are characteristic of all impact craters—the rim is higher than the surrounding land, and the crater bowl is below the level of the surrounding land. To me, Copernicus fits this description of an impact crater.

Green: When I look at the rays and smaller craters extending out from Copernicus Crater, I am reminded of the rifts, or cracks, that sometimes extend through volcanic areas, sometimes extending thousands of kilometers. These cracks allow molten material and gases to escape. It is possible that such cracks would be the sites of a number of smaller volcanic eruptions. The light-colored materials could be ash and dust released from the smaller volcanic craters along these rift lines.

Shoemaker: The rays extending out from Copernicus and the smaller craters are typical features of an impact. When nuclear bombs are set off a short distance underground the effect is a lot

CD-ROM

Moon binder/Geology/Craters on the Moon
- *Copernicus Crater Rays*
- *Bright-Rayed Crater*

like an impact. They produce craters. Material is launched into the air in great clumps. As the clumps fly through Earth's air, friction breaks them up. The ejected material falls back to Earth fairly uniformly.

On the Moon, where there is no atmosphere, the clumps fly out like streamers, settling to the surface in long lines called rays. Larger rocks in the ejecta strike the Moon's surface with enough force to form smaller, secondary craters.

Planetary Science Resources Book

page 21

CD-ROM

Earth binder/Geology/ Landforms on Earth
- *Mt. Saint Helens*

Green: If you visit any volcanic area on Earth, you see a lot of small craters around the site. These smaller craters are produced in a variety of ways. Some are produced by steam explosions, others by collapse of lava tubes, and still others by materials like volcanic bombs that are blasted out when the volcano explodes. These all produce many small craters. You really can't tell from a distance whether volcanoes produced these small craters or whether they were produced by a meteorite.

Planetary Science Resources Book

page 21

CD-ROM

Moon binder/Geology/Craters
- *Copernicus*
- *Copernicus (Apollo 12)*
- *Copernicus (Apollo 17)*
- *Copernicus Crater Rays*

Shoemaker: If you look around a volcano, you find that the small craters are just randomly spread around. With an impact crater, these smaller craters have a definite pattern. If we look around the large Copernicus Crater on the Moon, we see a pattern to the rays and these smaller craters. This pattern is in the shape of an arc. This is the kind of pattern formed from an impact by an object, throwing material out of the crater along a trajectory. We don't see these patterns around volcanoes.

Planetary Science Resources Book

page 21

CD-ROM

Moon binder/Geology/Craters on the Moon
- *Copernicus Crater (Apollo 17)*
- *Copernicus Crater Rays*
- *More about Copernicus*

Green: The small craters around Copernicus show up very clearly. I don't think these particular craters are of impact origin. To me, they appear to be volcanic. Some of these craters overlap. This type of overlapping crater is common on Earth in volcanic terrains. They're caused when the volcanic activity along a fracture shifts from one place to another. This leads me to the conclusion that the small craters around Copernicus are not of impact origin. I think they're volcanic. If this part of the area is volcanic, then all of Copernicus would have to have a volcanic origin.

CD-ROM

Moon binder/Geology/Moon Rocks and Minerals
• *Orange Moon Dust*

Shoemaker: When *Apollo 11* returned samples of lunar rocks and Moon soil, we discovered hardened lava, which we expected. However, there was also a large quantity of glass—tiny drops, spheres, and fragments. Microscopic inspection of the glass bits revealed tiny craters on the fragments, also lined with glass. The craters in some cases had tiny fragments of the meteorites that hit the glass. I conclude that these tiny craters are the products of impacts by minute particles flying through space, and that the same processes produced all the other craters as well, hundreds of meters and more in diameter. To me, this means that impacts have definitely changed the surface of the Moon.

CD-ROM

Earth binder/Geology/Earth Rocks and Minerals
• *Volcanic Ash*

Green: It is true that many of the glass spheres had been hit by tiny particles, as we expected we would find. Of greater interest to me is the fact that glass spheres and dumbbell-shaped pieces of glass, similar to those found on the Moon, are found on Earth in volcanic ash. For me it all fits together—the things we see, the similarity of the lunar features to volcanic features here on Earth, and the samples returned by the astronauts. The beauty of it all is that it can be explained by one well-understood natural process: volcanism.

CD-ROM

Moon binder/Geology/Craters on the Moon
• *Copernicus Crater Rays*

Shoemaker: One way to settle the controversy would be to go to the central peaks of Copernicus Crater. If my hypothesis is right, the peaks will be composed of large masses of rock brought up from depths within the Moon, heavily damaged by shock forces.

CD-ROM

Moon binder/Geology/Craters on the Moon
• *Copernicus Crater Rays*

Green: One way to settle the controversy would be to go to the central peaks of Copernicus Crater. If Copernicus is a caldera, I would expect the peaks to be composed of ordinary volcanic rock, unstressed by impact.

CRATERS: REAL AND SIMULATED

What created the craters on the Moon? For a long time scientists were not sure. Was it primarily volcanic activity or impacts? In the debate from the early 1960s, Jack Green thought the craters were inactive volcanoes and Eugene Shoemaker thought the craters were scars created by objects that slammed into the Moon's surface. Both men agreed that they could decide for sure which process produced the craters if they could examine rocks from the central peaks in some of the larger craters.

The impact theory proposes that objects of many sizes hit the Moon to produce craters of various sizes. Orbiting around the Sun with us are countless small- and medium-size pieces of rock and metal called *meteoroids.* Some of these are as small as dust, and some are the size of cities. When a meteoroid hits something, it can create a crater. Tiny meteors make craters that are microscopic; large meteoroids can produce craters so large that a person couldn't cross one by walking all day and all night.

Between the orbits of Mars and Jupiter is a big band of asteroids orbiting the Sun. These asteroids are thought to be chunks of material left over from when planets formed in the Solar System. When asteroids smash into the Moon, huge impact craters result.

Occasionally icy objects, called comets, come whizzing through the inner Solar System. Comets orbit the Sun, but they spend most of their time way out beyond the outermost planets in the Solar System. A comet may take 50 or more years to complete one orbit. A comet might end up on a collision course with the Moon. A series of more than 20 fragments of comet Shoemaker-Levy 9 actually hit the planet Jupiter in 1994. If a meteoroid of this magnitude were to hit the Moon, the resulting crater would be a major feature on the Moon's surface, perhaps even large enough to be visible from Earth with the naked eye.

Scientists in laboratories and students in classrooms can simulate impacts in order to study crater formation. They might use sand or flour to simulate the Moon's surface and some marbles, rocks, or other projectiles to simulate meteoroids. The "meteoroids" can be dropped or fired into the surface material to create impacts. The resulting craters have the characteristic hole, rim, ejecta, and rays of natural craters, but one element in the simulation is lacking. Even when scientists fire objects into the soil with specially designed guns, the speed of the objects is far slower than the pieces of debris traveling through space. Therefore, the energy released in the laboratory or classroom at the moment of impact does not accurately represent what really happens when a meteoroid slams into the Moon.

When a meteoroid traveling 72,000 km/h (20 km/s) smacks the Moon, a tremendous amount of energy is released. Wild things happen. Often the force of the impact creates so much pressure and heat that the meteoroid vaporizes, explodes, and disappears. It is the *explosion* that creates the crater by blasting the soil away in all directions.

A better way to simulate crater formation would be to drop a bomb into a large expanse of sand, or to place a firecracker in a box of flour. These experiments are not, however, recommended as classroom activities.

Small explosions produce small bowl-shaped craters with a fairly uniform blanket of ejecta distributed around the rim. These are **simple craters.**

A cluster of simple craters

Larger explosions produce so much pressure below the point of the impact that there is a rebound effect in the center of the crater. The shock wave pushing back up after the explosion often pushes up a big mountain in

the middle of the crater. **Complex craters** often have central peaks and ejecta thrown out in long rays.

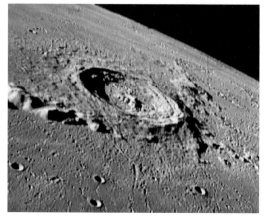

A typical complex crater with central peak

Really big complex craters have an additional feature—**terraces**—looking like giant steps leading from the crater floor up to the rim.

A large terraced crater

Think Question
Here is a view over the rim of a crater on the Moon. Which of the three crater classes does this one fall into? Why do you think so?

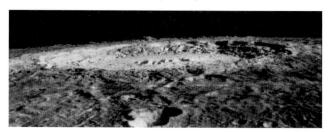

Compare Moon Craters with Classroom Craters

In class you have been simulating the formation of craters on the Moon by dropping marbles into flour. You produced craters, similar in many ways to those seen on the Moon. How are these craters actually like real Moon craters, and how are they different?

Size of crater: Your craters are 2–3 cm in diameter. The smallest Moon craters are microscopic. The largest one, the Aitken Basin at the Moon's south pole, is 2500 km across and 13 km deep—the biggest known impact crater in the Solar System! Imbrium Basin, another large impact crater, is 1200 km across.

Size of projectile: Your marbles are approximately 1.5 cm in diameter. Scientists believe the asteroid that collided with the Moon to create the Imbrium Basin was 100 km in diameter, but the chunks that made the craters on the Moon came in a wide range of sizes.

Speed of projectiles: Dropped from a height of 200 cm, or 2 m, your marbles reach a speed of perhaps 1 km/h. The asteroids and meteoroids that struck the Moon would have been traveling at speeds in the neighborhood of 20 km/s, or 72,000 km/h! Unlike Earth, the Moon has no atmosphere to slow a meteoroid down as it approaches the surface.

Impact event: When your marbles strike the flour, there is a "splash" of flour sprayed out across the surface of the pan. On the Moon, due to the speed and energy of large meteoroids, the impact is an explosive event. The heat generated by the impact is so intense that the rock instantly vaporizes. The resulting explosion caused by expanding gases excavates a huge hole and throws debris in all directions. This is how an object only 100 km across can create a crater with a diameter of 1200 km.

Lunar Regolith

For decades planetary scientists puzzled over the character of the Moon's surface. Many suspected that the Moon was covered in a thick layer of fine dust created as a result of millions of years of continuous pounding by countless meteoroids of all sizes. Some scientists proposed that the dust was light and airy, unable to support even the lightest weight. Those who believed the light-dust theory were afraid that a landing vehicle would simply disappear if it tried to land on the Moon's surface.

Other planetary scientists believed that the fine powder was densely packed, like powdered sugar or flour, and that people and lunar landers would stand and move around on it with ease, producing only shallow footprints.

Until probes equipped with video equipment were sent to the Moon for a look, it was impossible, even with the most powerful telescopes, to see enough detail to determine the characteristics of the surface with any degree of certainty. But the first probes clearly showed a lunar surface littered with large rocks, and when *Surveyor 1* landed on the Moon and trained its camera on its own landing pad, scientists clearly saw that the weight of the lander was easily supported by the compact lunar surface.

We now know that the surface of the Moon is covered with a relatively thin layer (2 to 20 m thick) of extremely fine rocky material called **lunar regolith** (*rego-* meaning "blanket" or "rug," and *lith-* meaning "rock"). The Moon is covered in a powdery blanket of pulverized rock.

The regolith is sometimes referred to as lunar soil. This is OK, but technically there is no soil on the Moon because one essential ingredient is missing. Soil is a mixture of mineral and organic material, like dead leaves, branches, and insects. Obviously there is no organic material on the Moon to produce a proper soil by Earth standards.

Think Questions

The photo to the left is a crater on Earth. Think about how it might have formed.

Is it a simple or complex crater?

How old do you think it might be? Why?

Why do you think there are so few craters on Earth, and so many on the Moon?

The Crater That Ended the Reign of the Dinosaurs

Back in the 1970s, a scientist named Dr. Walter Alverez was investigating sedimentary rocks on a mountainside in Italy. Sedimentary rocks form when layers of sand, dust, clay, and ash pile up and, over time, are transformed into rock. What Alverez found was an unusually high concentration of a rare element called iridium. While iridium is rare on Earth's surface, he knew that one source of iridium was the meteorites and asteroids that hit Earth from time to time. Alverez began to wonder if the layer of iridium he discovered in the rocks could be asteroid or meteorite dust.

Back in the laboratory, further analysis revealed that the thin layer of rock in which the iridium occurred was 65 million years old. Thus, Alverez reasoned, there might have been a big comet or asteroid impact on Earth 65 million years ago that accounted for the iridium in his rock samples.

But Alverez and his research group still had more questions. They wondered if an iridium layer would be found in 65-million-year-old sedimentary rocks from other places on Earth. When they looked, they did find high concentrations of iridium in 65-million-year-old rocks in many other places around the planet. Now they wondered what process or processes might have resulted in the layering of iridium into rocks all over Earth at the same time. The answer that they came up with was one huge impact that blasted a huge amount of dust into the atmosphere. The dust circled the globe for a long time, carried by circulating winds. The dust, including iridium from the asteroid that exploded, settled out of the atmosphere, all over the planet.

The other interesting event that happened at the same time involves dinosaurs (and many other kinds of plants and animals). For years paleontologists (scientists who study fossils) had known that many species of dinosaurs disappeared from Earth about 65 million years ago. Alverez and his group wondered if the extinction of the dinosaurs and the suspected asteroid impact could be related. How could one asteroid impact cause the extinction of dinosaurs all over the world?

Alverez's group, and other groups of scientists, worked up some scientific models that suggested that an asteroid about 10 km across could throw enough material into the atmosphere to obscure the Sun for a year. If this happened, much of the plant life on Earth would die from lack of solar energy, and the foundation for the food chain would fail. With a large percentage of the food removed from the planet, many species would starve to death outright, or their vitality would be reduced so that the result would be a gradual but steady decline toward extinction.

There was one problem, however. A 10-km asteroid would produce a crater at least 100 km across, and search as geologists would, they could find no evidence of such a crater. Many suggested that the impact site might be hidden under the sea, which covers about two-thirds of the planet's surface.

What do you think? Does it seem reasonable that a huge Earth impact did occur 65 million years ago? If so, where do you think the impact might have occurred?

Since geologists first mounted a search for the impact crater that killed the dinosaurs, new technologies have emerged. Scientists now have advanced X-ray scanners that can "see" through water to look for obscure, ancient features of the land. An interesting structure was discovered in the Gulf of Mexico. This is an image of that structure.

This murky image may not look like much to the untrained eye, but now that you have studied craters and know what to look for, you can see the distinctive shapes that suggest a crater.

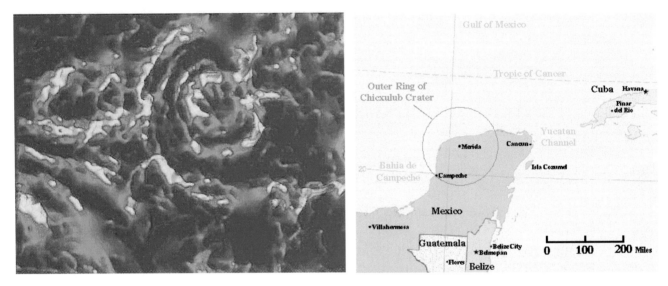

This structure is named Chicxulub Crater, located just off the tip of the Yucatan Peninsula of Mexico in the Gulf of Mexico. The crater is huge—the size predicted by the Alverez team. It represented the size of impact that would be needed to cause the extinctions described above. What do you think? Could the dust and smoke thrown into the atmosphere from the impact that made this buried crater have darkened the skies for months, killing many plants and animals?

Think Questions

What kinds of animals might have survived the period of reduced light?

If a massive impact like the Chicxulub impact were to happen today, what might be the result worldwide?

Look at the outer ring of the Chicxulub Crater in the illustration above. How destructive would that crater be in your area? Get a local map and position a model of the crater in your area to get an idea of the massive size of this event.

HOW TO GET AND HOLD ONTO A MOON

Counting out from the Sun, our planet, Earth, is the first one keeping company with a satellite, or moon. Mercury, the closest planet to the Sun, doesn't have a moon, nor does Venus. Mars, the fourth planet out, has two moons, but they are really just a couple of Mars's big old rocks that probably ended up in orbit after they were fully formed. And it is suspected that Earth didn't have a moon at first, but acquired one early in its history as a result of a gigantic planetary collision. Visualize the event as it may have happened perhaps 4.5 billion years ago.

Earth was pretty much formed as a planet. Most of the dust and gas in the region had been pulled in, and the proto-Earth was revolving around the Sun more or less in the orbit it travels today. However, these were the early days of the Solar System, and if you looked around, you would surely have noticed a lot of renegade material flying around in unstable orbits. Some of the chunks were huge—the size of small planets themselves.

Planetary scientists now think that one of these large planetesimals, perhaps the size of Mars, was traveling around the Sun in an exaggerated elliptical orbit. It's not known why it had such a peculiar orbit—perhaps it was pulled by the gravitational influence of a large planet, or perhaps there were lots of objects following dangerous paths early in the Solar System's history. Anyway, it ended up heading for Earth.

Had you been on Earth to witness the event, the troublemaker would have first appeared as a dot in the heavens. Over a period of days and weeks it would grow bigger and bigger until it completely filled the field of view above Earth in that direction. Then it struck. Because the colliding objects were so large, the impact itself seemed to happen in slow motion, lasting several minutes, even though the planetesimal was traveling at perhaps 40,000 km/h.

But what chaos followed the crash! First of all, the incoming object apparently was destroyed on impact. The planetesimal was reduced to vapor, dust, and chunks, with any surviving parts being driven deep into the interior of Earth. A significant portion of Earth was disintegrated as well. The energy that resulted from the crash produced an explosion of unimaginable magnitude. Earth itself might have been in danger of being blasted apart.

The explosive release of energy threw a tremendous quantity of matter into motion—probably at least 20 billion cubic kilometers of matter. One portion of the matter, the most energized pieces of debris, flew out into space, never to be seen again. Another portion of the matter flew up into the air and then returned to Earth, some almost immediately as huge rocks, some a little later as granules of various sizes, and some months or even years later in the form of dust and chemicals held aloft in the atmosphere.

A third and significant portion of the debris didn't fly off into space and it didn't return to Earth. It began orbiting the Earth in a disk, rather like the rings of Saturn. The ring was probably about two Earth diameters from the surface of Earth. Over the next millions of years the pieces of matter and dust started to attract one another, gradually forming larger and larger chunks, which eventually formed our Moon.

We had a Moon where previously there was none, and it must have been a sight hanging up there maybe 30,000 km above Earth, rather than the 385,000 km distance we see today.

The Role of Gravity in Moon Behavior

Gravity is one of the four known forces in the universe. Gravity, along with electromagnetism and two forces at work inside the structure of atoms, makes everything in the world behave in ways we understand. Gravity is the force that causes two masses to attract one another. The force of gravity exerted by a small mass, like a marble or an apple, is so small that we can't detect it. But the gravity exerted by a large mass, like a planet or a star, is tremendous. The larger the mass, the stronger the force of gravity it exerts.

When the planetesimal hit Earth, some matter was thrown straight up in the air. There were two possible fates for that matter. If it were launched with sufficient velocity, it might escape Earth's gravity and begin a phase of existence as loose space debris. If it didn't achieve escape velocity, Earth's gravity would pull it back down to the surface. It's just that simple.

However, most of the matter ejected by the impact would not go straight up, but would be launched at an angle. Something different could happen to this matter.

Before we get into where that matter went, consider another piece of information about the behavior of matter. Isaac Newton figured out that an object in motion will travel in a straight line until it is acted on by a force that changes its direction. In other words, things don't travel in curves, circles, spirals, zigzags, or any other nonstraight paths unless something acts on them to change their motion.

Back to the impact debris. The matter flying out from the impact at an angle, in a straight line, will be acted on by Earth's gravity. Take a rock the size of a television set as an example. It flies off in a straight line, but at an angle. If there were no gravity, the rock would just keep going. But there is gravity, and it pulls on the rock, bringing it back to Earth. But the rock is going sideways so fast that the pull only changes the direction of the rock as it moves. Remember, the rock travels in a straight line until acted on by a force, and the force changing the rock's direction in this case is Earth's gravity.

Imagine taking a yo-yo by the end of its string and swinging it around over your head. You have it going in a nice circle. If you let go of the string, what happens? It stops going in a circle and flies off in a straight line. As long as you keep applying a force (pulling on the string) to change the direction of the yo-yo, it continues to orbit your fist.

Gravity is the "string" pulling on the Moon to keep it in a circular path. Similarly, gravity is the force keeping Earth (as well as the other planets) in a circular orbit around the Sun. In fact, everything that is behaving in a predictable way in the Solar System is orbiting something else, and in every case gravity rules the action.

Eugene M. Shoemaker, Planetary Scientist
(April 28, 1928 – July 18, 1997)

Eugene "Gene" Merle Shoemaker was a planetary scientist who specialized in meteor impacts and the role they have played in the Solar System. His passion was astrogeology, and he dreamed of going to the Moon. Almost single-handedly he created the discipline of planetary geology as distinct from astronomy.

He died on July 18, 1997, in a car accident while hunting for meteor craters in Australia. Gene Shoemaker had become well known to the Australians, and wherever he went, he captivated people's imaginations with his all-encompassing enthusiasm for geology, love of the land, and warm personality.

Gene Shoemaker's claim to fame was his pioneering research on the formation of impact craters on the Moon as well as on Earth and other planetary bodies, and his discovery of numerous Earth-crossing asteroids and comets. Gene, who along with his wife, Carolyn, and a colleague, David Levy, is best known for discovering comet Shoemaker-Levy 9, whose pieces crashed into Jupiter in July 1994. Together, the Shoemakers were the leading discoverers of comets in this century, and are credited with discovering more than 800 asteroids.

Gene Shoemaker seems to have been a geologist from the day he was born in Los Angeles, in 1928. He graduated from the California Institute of Technology in Pasadena at the age of 19, and completed a master's degree only a year later. He joined the U.S. Geological Survey and began exploring for uranium deposits in Colorado and Utah in 1948. These studies brought him near many volcanic features and the one impact crater on the Colorado Plateau in the western United States, namely Hopi Buttes and Barringer Crater (also known as Meteor Crater).

In 1957–1960 Shoemaker carried out pioneering work on the nature and origin of Barringer Crater (near Winslow, Arizona), which provided a foundation for crater research on the Moon and planets. At this time Shoemaker and his colleague E. C. T. Chao discovered coesite, a mineral created *only* during impacts, in the rubble at the bottom of Barringer Crater. This mineral provided geologists with a fingerprint to look for when investigating structures that might be ancient impact craters elsewhere on Earth. Soon thereafter Shoemaker found coesite in the Ries Basin in Germany, proving that it was in fact a giant impact structure, the second confirmed Earth crater to be discovered. The discovery of coesite provided the tool geologists needed to identify many more impact structures on Earth, and eventually led to the theory that catastrophic impacts may have caused mass extinctions over geological time.

A man of vision, Gene Shoemaker believed geological studies would be extended into space, and in his early career, he dreamed of being the first geologist to map the Moon. However, a health problem prevented Shoemaker from being the first astronaut geologist. Even so, he personally helped train the Apollo astronauts and sat beside Walter Cronkite in the evening news, giving geological commentary during the historic Moon walks—walks that he would have taken, had things worked out a little differently.

During the 1960s Shoemaker led teams that investigated the structure and history of the

Moon and developed methods of planetary geological mapping using telescope images of the Moon. He was involved in the Ranger and Surveyor Moon-probe programs, continued with the manned Apollo programs, and culminated his Moon studies in 1994 as science team leader for the Clementine project.

Gene Shoemaker was a very highly respected scientist. The University of Arizona awarded him an honorary doctorate of science in 1984. In 1992 he received the National Medal of Science from President George Bush, the highest scientific honor given in the United States.

From the time he was a teenager, Shoemaker wanted to go to the Moon. He told friends that his inability to qualify for astronaut training was his greatest personal regret. Shortly before Shoemaker died, he said, "Not going to the Moon and banging on it with my own hammer has been the biggest disappointment in life."

In death Gene Shoemaker realized his life's great ambition. His colleagues and friends, acknowledging his passion to travel to the Moon, placed a small polycarbonate capsule carrying an ounce of his cremated remains in the *Lunar Prospector* spacecraft. The capsule, 4.5 cm long and 1.8 cm in diameter, was carried in a vacuum sealed, flight-tested aluminum sleeve mounted deep inside the spacecraft.

Around the capsule was wrapped a piece of brass foil inscribed with an image of comet Hale-Bopp, an image of Meteor Crater in Arizona, and a passage from Shakespeare's enduring love story, *Romeo and Juliet*.

When the tiny *Lunar Prospector* crashed into a dark crater near the Moon's south pole on Saturday, August 31, 1999, it deposited the

EUGENE M. SHOEMAKER
1928-1997

And, when he shall die,
Take him and cut him out in little stars,
And he will make the face of heaven so fine
That all the world will be in love with night,
And pay no worship to the garish sun.

— William Shakespeare
'Romeo and Juliet', 1595

ashes of the pioneering astrogeologist on the lunar surface. There could be no finer tribute to the legendary planetary geologist who said his greatest unfulfilled dream was to go to the Moon.

And, when he shall die,
Take him and cut him out in little stars,
And he will make the face of heaven so fine
That all the world will be in love with night,
And pay no worship to the garish sun.

William Shakespeare, Romeo and Juliet

Tribute design by Carolyn C. Porco

Lunar Probes: Paving the Way for Apollo

After President John F. Kennedy made his bold statement on May 25, 1961, proclaiming to the world that the United States would send men to the Moon by the end of the decade, Moon exploration got serious. There was a lot to learn before a mission could be launched with any hope for success. To get the information, NASA launched three programs, each developing a different kind of probe. The three programs were known as **Ranger, Surveyor,** *and* **Lunar Orbiter.**

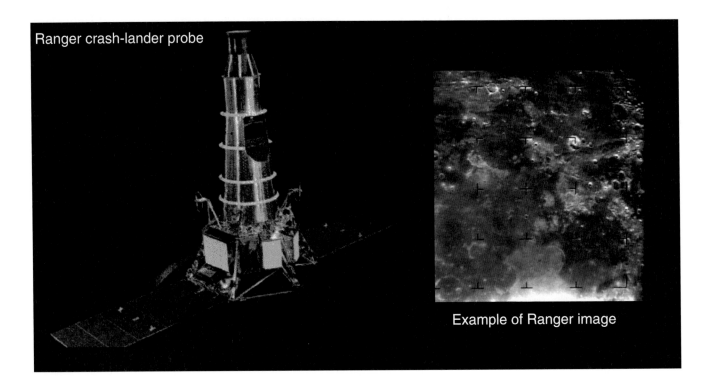

Ranger crash-lander probe

Example of Ranger image

Ranger

Ranger was the first program to fly. It was basically designed as a platform for television cameras intended to get close-up pictures of the Moon's surface. The method was straightforward: fly directly into the Moon, sending pictures back to Earth right up until the probe plowed into the lunar surface. The program launched nine Rangers. The first two, launched in 1961, were test vehicles, not intended to go to the Moon. *Rangers 3, 4,* and *5,* launched in 1962, were intended to test the cameras and check out the guidance systems. *Ranger 3* missed the Moon altogether, and *Rangers 4* and *5* failed before even one image was sent to Earth.

The final four Rangers were launched in 1964 and 1965. *Ranger 6* failed, but *Rangers 7, 8,* and *9* performed perfectly. Each kamikaze probe bristled with six cameras, some designed for wide-angle shots, others for close-ups. The images of the Moon provided NASA with views 1000 times sharper than had ever been seen before. *Ranger 7* struck mare terrain covered by crater rays. *Ranger 8* also struck mare terrain, which has a complex system of ridges. *Ranger 9* hit in a large crater in the lunar highlands. One thing these highly detailed images showed Apollo planners was that finding a smooth, level landing site was not going to be easy.

Surveyor

Next up was the Surveyor program with seven probes also destined for the lunar surface. However, the Surveyors were designed to soft land and report back to NASA engineers what it was like to be on the Moon's surface. So many questions would be answered if the missions were successful. What does the surface look like up close? How solid is it? Will it support the weight of a person or a machine? What kind of material is on the surface of the Moon? Is it flat anywhere on the Moon?

The first of the five successful Surveyor missions was launched on May 31, 1966, and the program continued until January 1968. They were pretty big spacecraft, each weighing in at 1000 kg, and measuring 3.3 m high, and 4.5 m in diameter. Part of the probe's bulk was attributed to the hardware and fuel required for a soft landing.

The gentle touchdown was achieved by firing rocket engines to slow the rate of descent. The probe was barely moving when it settled onto the lunar surface, perched on its tripod landing gear.

Some of the Surveyors just took pictures— pictures of unparalleled quality and resolution. Others sent back information about the magnetic properties of the surface, the temperature, and the chemical composition of the surface material. Most important, however, was the information sent back when a little scooper/ digger device, rather like a tiny backhoe, dug into the lunar regolith. The sides of the trench it dug did not collapse or crumble, demonstrating that the surface material would hold together and support the weight of people and landing vehicles in the not-too-distant future.

Surveyor space probe—a soft lander

Lunar Orbiter

Eastern Sea

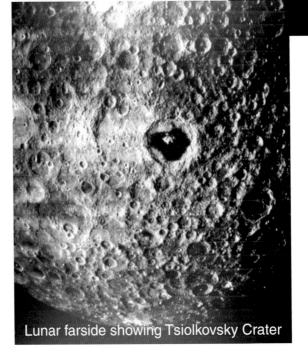

Lunar farside showing Tsiolkovsky Crater

Lunar Orbiter

Last to get started by a few months was the Lunar Orbiter program, initiated in August 1966. The plan called for five identical 390-kg spacecraft to be placed into orbit around the Moon to look for smooth, level areas on the Moon's nearside suitable for manned landing sites for the Apollo program. In addition to the photography, the missions would gather important information about the Moon's gravity and the potential hazards posed by micrometeoroids (which could punch a hole in a spacecraft) and radiation intensities.

These early orbiting probes took photographs using cameras and film, just like you might use to take pictures of a picnic in the park with friends. Unlike Earth-based photography, however, the Lunar Orbiter was equipped with an automatic system for developing the film, scanning the image from the film, digitizing the image, and sending the information back to Earth. The NASA engineers felt that was the best way to get high-resolution images for careful study.

During the first three missions, 20 potential lunar landing sites were photographed from low-altitude orbits. From these, eight promising sites were selected. The fourth and fifth missions were devoted to broader scientific objectives. The entire nearside of the Moon and 95% of the farside were photographed from high-altitude orbit.

Lunar Orbiter was equipped to take medium-resolution photographs and high-resolution photographs at the same time. These two images of Tycho Crater show examples of these two views.

Tycho—medium resolution   *Tycho—high resolution*

In addition, Lunar Orbiter could look to the horizon for a long-distance view, as demonstrated in this photo of the Marius Hills in the Ocean of Storms.

Marius Hills in Oceanus Procellarum.

The accumulated information and imagery provided by these three space-probe programs prepared NASA to land the *Eagle* on the Moon in July 1969. Each program added a little more to our knowledge of the Moon. Without the close, detailed images and scientific information provided by these mechanical extensions of our senses, the manned trip to the Moon would not have been possible. The preparation paid off. We made it to the Moon. So, where do you think humans will park their spaceship next? And what kinds of information will we need to have before we take off on the next leg of the space adventure?

Think Question

Why do you think the lunar-probe programs focused so much attention on the nearside of the Moon?

Top Ten Scientific Discoveries Made during Apollo Exploration of the Moon

1.

The Moon is not a primordial object; it is an evolved terrestrial planet with internal zoning similar to that of Earth.

Before Apollo, the state of the Moon was a subject of almost unlimited speculation. We now know that the Moon is made of rocky material that has been variously melted, erupted through volcanoes, and crushed by meteoroid impacts. The Moon possesses a thick crust (60 km), a fairly uniform lithosphere (60–1000 km), and a partly liquid asthenosphere (1000–1740 km). A small iron core at the bottom of the asthenosphere is possible but unconfirmed. Some rocks give hints of ancient magnetic fields, although no planetary field exists today.

2.

The Moon is ancient and still preserves an early history (the first billion years) that must be common to all terrestrial planets.

The extensive record of impact craters on the Moon, when calibrated using absolute ages of rock samples, provides a key for unravelling time scales for the geologic evolution of Mercury, Venus, and Mars based on their individual crater records. Photogeologic interpretation of other planets is based on lessons learned from the Moon. Before Apollo, the origin of lunar impact craters was not fully understood and the origin of similar craters on Earth was highly debated.

3.

The youngest Moon rocks are virtually as old as the oldest Earth rocks. The earliest processes and events that probably affected both planetary bodies can now be found only on the Moon.

Moon rock ages range from about 3.2 billion years in the maria (dark, low basins) to nearly 4.6 billion years in the terrae (light, rugged highlands). Active geologic forces, including plate tectonics and erosion, continuously repave the oldest surfaces on Earth, whereas old surfaces persist with little disturbance on the Moon.

4.

The Moon and Earth are genetically related and formed from different proportions of a common reservoir of materials.

The distinctively similar oxygen isotopic compositions of Moon rocks and Earth rocks clearly show common ancestry. Relative to Earth, however, the Moon was highly depleted in iron and in volatile elements that are needed to form atmospheric gases and water.

5.

The Moon is lifeless; it contains no living organisms, fossils, or organic compounds.

Extensive testing revealed no evidence for life, past or present, among the lunar samples. Even nonbiological organic compounds are amazingly absent; traces can be attributed to contamination by meteoroids.

6.

All Moon rocks originated through high-temperature processes with little or no involvement with water. They are roughly divisible into three types: basalts, anorthosites, and breccias.

Basalts are dark lava rocks that fill mare basins; they generally resemble, but are much older than, lavas that make up the oceanic crust of Earth. Anorthosites are light rocks that form the ancient highlands; they generally resemble, but are much older than, the most ancient rocks on Earth. Breccias are composite rocks formed from all other rock types through crushing, mixing, and sintering during impact events. The Moon has no sandstones, shales, or limestones such as testify to the importance of water-borne processes on Earth.

7. **Early in its history, the Moon was melted to great depths to form a "magma ocean." The lunar highlands contain the remnants of early, low-density rocks that floated to the surface of the magma ocean.**

The lunar highlands were formed about 4.4–4.6 billion years ago by flotation of an early, feldspar-rich crust on a magma ocean that covered the Moon to a depth of many tens of kilometers or more. Innumerable meteoroid impacts through geologic time reduced much of the ancient crust to arcuate mountain ranges between basins.

8. **The lunar magma ocean was followed by a series of huge asteroid impacts that created basins, which were later filled by lava flows.**

The large, dark basins, such as Mare Imbrium [the Sea of Rains], are gigantic impact craters, formed early in lunar history, that were later filled by lava flows about 3.2–3.9 billion years ago. Lunar volcanism occurred mostly as lava floods that spread horizontally; volcanic fire fountains produced deposits of orange and emerald green glass beads.

9. **The Moon is slightly asymmetrical in bulk form, possibly as a consequence of its evolution under Earth's gravitational influence. Its crust is thicker on the farside, while most volcanic basins—and unusual mass concentrations—occur on the nearside.**

Mass is not distributed uniformly inside the Moon. Large mass concentrations (Mascons) lie beneath the surface of many large lunar basins and probably represent thick accumulations of dense lava. Relative to its geometric center, the Moon's center of mass is displaced toward Earth by several kilometers.

10. **The surface of the Moon is covered by a rubble pile of rock fragments and dust, called the lunar regolith, that contains a unique radiation history of the Sun, which is of importance to understanding climate changes on Earth.**

The regolith was produced by innumerable meteoroid impacts through geologic time. Surface rocks and mineral grains are distinctively enriched in chemical elements and isotopes implanted by solar radiation. As such, the Moon has recorded 4 billion years of the Sun's history to a degree of completeness that we are unlikely to find elsewhere.

The Lunar Quest Continues

More than 60 research laboratories throughout the world continue studies on the Apollo lunar samples. Many new analytical technologies, which did not exist in 1969–72 when the Apollo missions were returning lunar samples to Earth, are now being applied by a third generation of scientists. The deepest secrets of the Moon remain to be revealed.

Reproduced courtesy of NASA Apollo Manned Space Program

The Search for New Moons

The universe is full of heavenly bodies that inspire poets and intrigue scientists.

By Robert S. Boyd
Reprinted with permission of Knight Ridder/Tribune
Information Services

Washington

Here's a trivia question sure to stump your friends: How many moons are there in our solar system?

It's a rare person who knows the answer: 63 moons and climbing.

In September 1997, two more satellites were discovered circling counterclockwise around Uranus, the seventh planet from the Sun.

"It's almost inconceivable there aren't more moons out there," said Brett Gladman, an astronomer currently working at the Observatoire de la Côte d'Azur in France, who detected the new Uranian moons. "Almost every time there is an advance in detector efficiency, we find more satellites."

The search for new moons—as well as planets, comets, asteroids, rocks and dust littering the starry skies—is part of humankind's age-old quest to understand the universe we live in.

By studying them, scientists have learned much about how the solar system, including Earth, formed and what its fate may be.

Besides, as poets, lovers and mystics know, moons are cool.

Earth and Pluto, the ninth planet, are the only members of our Sun's family to have just one

Asteroid Ida with satellite Dactyl

Mars' irregular moon Phobos

moon each. Mercury and Venus have none. But Mars has two, Jupiter 16, Saturn 18, Uranus 17, and Neptune eight.

Even a little asteroid, Ida, floating between Mars and Jupiter, has its own pet moonlet, named Dactyl, only 1 mile wide.

The giant planets—Jupiter, Saturn, Uranus, and Neptune—have so many moons that they resemble miniature solar systems. Astronomers have assigned them romantic names culled from Greek mythology and plays of Shakespeare: Atlas, Pandora, Ophelia, Ariel, Juliet and the like.

This burgeoning horde of satellites indicates that moons may be common around other planets in the universe, offering more potential habitat for life.

In the past three years, more than a dozen new planets, most of them more massive than Jupiter, have been discovered spinning around distant stars.

Although these planets are inhospitable for living creatures, at least like any on Earth, scientists say they might have livable moons.

"Giant planets do not offer good conditions for life, but moons around giant planets could have habitable zones," said Christopher Chyba, a planetary scientist at Stanford University. "There is reason to be optimistic about the number of worlds that could support life."

The moons in our solar system come in a rich variety of sizes, temperatures, atmospheres, and behaviors.

Mighty Jupiter boasts both the biggest and the smallest satellites so far. Little Leda is only 6 miles across, while Ganymede and Titan are actually bigger than two planets, Mercury and Pluto.

Titan is of special interest because of its atmosphere—a thick haze of hydrocarbons resembling Atlanta on a smoggy day—which

Saturn's moon Titan

warms the moon by the greenhouse effect. Astronomers believe sunlight is driving chemical reactions on Titan like those that preceded the formation of living molecules on Earth.

"Titan may be a model for early Earth," Chyba said. "Titan is the only example of a world where prebiotic chemistry is ongoing."

Although no one expects to find life on Saturn's Titan, some scientists think another of Jupiter's moons, Europa, has a vast ocean of water, 60 to 100 miles deep, beneath its icy surface that might harbor living microorganisms.

"There is overpowering evidence that Europa has—or used to have—a substantial ocean, more ocean water than on Earth," said Frank Carsey, a scientist at the National Aeronautics and Space Administration's Jet Propulsion Laboratory.

Water, along with a source of energy and the right mix of chemicals, is an essential ingredient of life. Europa has all three ingredients.

Jupiter's moon Europa

Nothing could live on Europa's frozen crust, however. Besides being bitterly cold, the moon is bathed in radiation.

NASA's spacecraft *Galileo* recently picked up evidence that Callisto, another of Jupiter's moons, may also have a subsurface ocean.

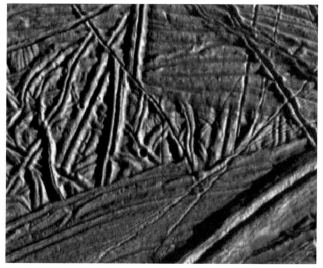

Close-up of Europa's surface

"Until now, we thought Callisto was a dead and boring moon, just a hunk of rock and ice," said Margaret Kivelson, a professor of space physics at the University of California at Los Angeles. "This new data suggests that something is hidden below Callisto's surface, and that something may very well be a salty ocean."

Unlike our own dead moon, some satellites lead active lives.

Io, a moon of Jupiter, is so volcanic that it "glows in the dark," said Paul Geissler, an astronomer at the University of Arizona in Tucson. A NASA photo caught one volcano in mid-eruption, shooting a plume of hot gas hundreds of miles into space.

"Io glows green, blue and red," said Geissler. "It looks like a Christmas tree, colorful and mysterious."

Moons also perform useful tasks, such as helping to preserve the shiny rings, composed of small rocks, dust, or ice, that surround some planets.

A ring around Uranus is shepherded by two moons, one on either side. Four of Jupiter's moons cling to the edge of that planet's faint rings. Saturn's gorgeous rings may also have shepherd moons, but they have not been detected yet.

Our own Moon probably deflected a number of asteroids that might have smashed into Earth, causing enormous damage. The huge craters on the Moon bear witness to its service as a shield for our planet.

In fact, some scientists believe our Moon was created when an object the size of Mars collided

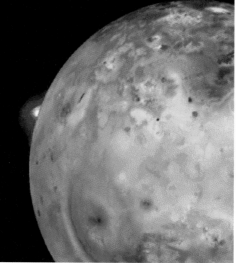
Jupiter's volcanic moon Io erupting

with Earth, hurling a huge mass of molten material into orbit.

One theory to explain why the giant planets have so many satellites, Gladman said, is that passing objects were trapped in their gravitational fields and could not escape. "This is all ancient history, from way back at the beginning of the solar system," he said.

In addition to the 63 moons, in the past six years astronomers have detected 64 miniature planets floating in the remote regions beyond Neptune. There are probably tens of thousands of these "Kuiper Belt objects," named for Dutch-born astronomer Gerard Kuiper, but they are so small—about 60 miles wide—and so distant they are extremely hard to see.

The exploration of the moons continues: Recent flybys of our own Moon turned up evidence of water, iron, and magnetic fields.

The *Galileo* spacecraft is collecting more detailed images of Jupiter's satellites. NASA's Cassini mission to Saturn will drop a probe onto the surface of Titan in 2004.

A visit to Pluto and its moon, Charon, is proposed early in the next century. The space agency is planning a robotic landing on Europa to confirm that it has an ocean.

"We expect one day to penetrate the ocean of Europa," said Roger Kern, a Jet Propulsion Laboratory biologist. "Not long ago, this was more fanciful than real. Now it's more real than fanciful."

Solar System Moon Count

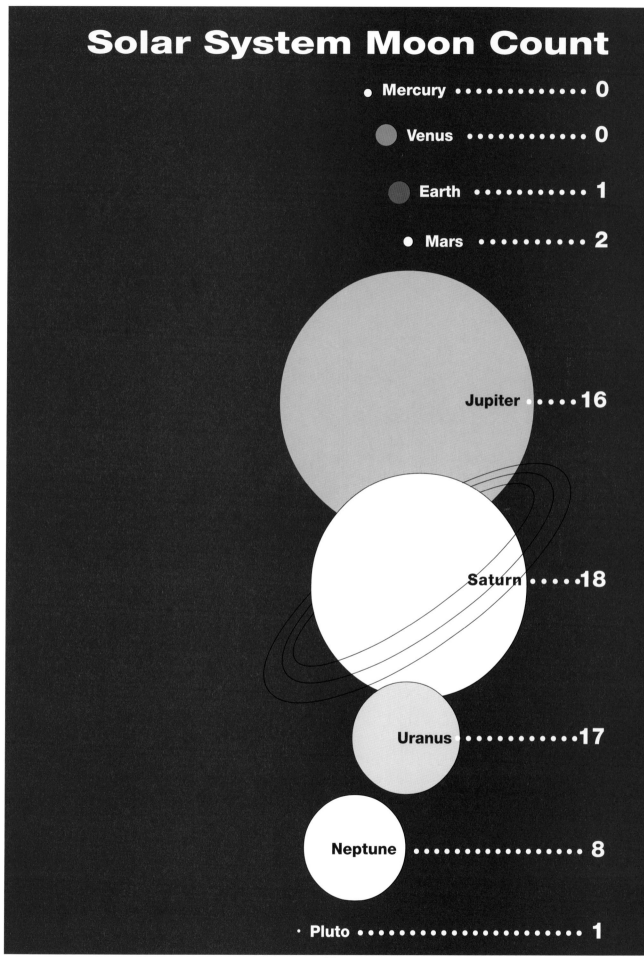

Mercury • • • • • • • • • • • • 0

Venus • • • • • • • • • • • 0

Earth • • • • • • • • • • 1

Mars • • • • • • • • • • 2

Jupiter • • • • • • 16

Saturn • • • • • 18

Uranus • • • • • • • • • • • 17

Neptune • • • • • • • • • • • • • • 8

Pluto • • • • • • • • • • • • • • • • • 1

THE SOLAR SYSTEM IN A NUTSHELL

A lot is known about the **Solar System.** We know how big it is, about how old it is, a lot about the distribution of matter in it, and a good bit about how the pieces move around. This article is a short review of the knowledge of the Solar System that has been accumulated over the centuries by thousands of curious humans.

Something over 4.5 billion years ago a modest accumulation of dust and gases in our part of the **Milky Way** galaxy began to draw together as a result of gravity. As the vast cloud, known as the **solar nebula,** condensed, it began to spin and flatten into a disk, like a huge phonograph record. Most of the matter was drawn into the center of the vortex, but not all of it. In several places away from the center, smaller accumulations of dust and gas began to spin. This was the situation as the Solar System was in its early stages of formation—a kind of cosmic carousel at least 10 billion kilometers in

diameter, spinning around a massive center, with smaller whirligigs circling the center at various distances.

Just about all the matter in the Solar System gravitated to the center and became the **Sun.** The Sun accounts for about 99.8% of the mass of the system. The 0.2% that was not drawn into the Sun formed nine planets, several dozen moons, and a collection of lesser objects like asteroids, comets, and unincorporated debris out on the fringes of the Solar System.

The Sun rules. Because of its mass, it exerts a mighty gravitational force on all the other members of the system, and it is responsible for maintaining the orbits of the planets. Also, during the Sun's formative phase its gravity powerfully condensed and compressed the hydrogen and other gases. Things got hotter and hotter until a thermonuclear reaction began. Hydrogen began to fuse into helium at a furious rate, releasing huge quantities of energy. The Sun "turned on," and a star was born.

While the Sun was condensing, so were the smaller accumulations of matter orbiting around it. These nine (or more) spinning locations became the planets.

The planets were undoubtedly formed from the same raw materials as the Sun, but they are quite different in properties. The four planets closest to the Sun are known as the **terrestrial planets.** They are often considered together because of their similarities. Today they are all composed primarily of rock and metal and have solid surfaces and gaseous atmospheres of various densities and compositions. The four terrestrial planets are all relatively close to the Sun; light reaches Mars, the fourth planet out, just 12.6 minutes after it leaves the Sun.

It is believed that the four terrestrial planets formed in a long and violent process of condensation, gravitational attraction, and collisions. Because the action took place so close to the Sun, the lighter, more volatile materials, like water, nitrogen, carbon dioxide, hydrogen, and helium, did not condense, but were driven away from the developing planets. The rocky and metallic matter collected into larger and larger objects. Eventually they sorted themselves out into the four planets closest to the Sun.

These planets are small. The combination of heat (generated by collisions and the Sun) and the weak gravitational attraction of the small planets made it impossible for them to attract and hold the lighter, more volatile materials, such as gases and water. The

terrestrial planets formed without atmospheres and without volatile materials.

Planetary scientists think that it was some time after the terrestrial planets formed that they acquired atmospheres as a result of gases and water escaping from the interiors of the planets (out-gassing through volcanism) and bombardment by water-rich comets. The evolution and fates of these volatile materials varied from planet to planet, resulting in the unique family of inner planets we see today.

Gas Giants

Planets 5–8 are the four **gas giants.** They are truly huge compared to the little terrestrials closer to the Sun. And they are considerably farther from the Sun; light reaches Jupiter, the fifth planet out, 43 minutes after leaving the Sun, and Neptune, the eighth planet out, receives light 4.2 hours after it leaves the Sun.

At these distances from the Sun, the more volatile materials did condense and become part of the planetary mass, including ice. Because the gas giants acquired so much matter, their gravity was powerful enough to hold the volatile materials, especially the gases hydrogen and helium. In fact, the gravitational compression of gases in the giants was so intense that they began to heat up, starting a process like the one that led to the formation of the Sun. However, because they are way too small to develop the internal pressures needed to start the thermonuclear star process, they may have simply glowed red for a few years before cooling off.

What about little Pluto, whose origin and even status as planet, are subjects of ongoing discussion? More on it later. But first, a brief visit to each planet in the Solar System, starting with Mercury, closest planet to the Sun.

Mercury

Mercury is a small, barren planet. It has no water, almost no atmosphere (a little sodium and potassium vapor), and no moons. Mercury's surface is heavily cratered, still bearing the scars of the violent history that hammered all of the planets billions of years ago. Many of the craters are flooded with lava, like the Moon.

Mercury has the most extreme temperature fluctuations of all the planets, ranging from over 400°C during the day to below –180° at night. Mercury turns on its axis very slowly, taking 59 Earth days to make a complete rotation. Thus the Mercury day is 59 days long. Mercury revolves around the Sun in just 88 Earth days, however, so a year on Mercury is just a little longer than a day.

Venus

Venus is number 2, a planet that appears to be Earth's twin in size and material. But conditions on the two planets are very different. Venus has a dense atmosphere composed mostly of carbon dioxide and sulfuric acid. The atmospheric pressure at the surface of the planet is crushing—100 times that found on Earth's surface. It wasn't until 1990, when planetary scientists began getting radar data from the *Magellan* space probe, that they were able to view the surface of Venus. They discovered that 85% of the surface is rock, much of it lava flows. The rest is mountainous, with a number of impact craters in evidence. The relatively low density of craters, however, and the low rate of erosion, suggest that the entire surface of Venus was "repaved" some time after the early period of bombardment.

Venus rotates on its axis in the opposite direction from Earth, so a typical sunrise (if you could see the Sun) would occur in the west, and the Sun would set in the east. And rotation is slow. A Venusian day is 243 Earth days long, but Venus revolves around the Sun in 226 days. Yes, it is true that the day on Venus is longer than the year.

Because of the dense atmosphere, heat gets trapped on Venus, raising the temperature at the planet's surface to 484°C. And the insulating effect of the atmosphere prevents the planet from cooling down during the night. Venus is a hot planet.

Earth

The third rocky planet from the Sun is our blue oasis in space. Earth is a water planet, and the temperature fluctuation, which is just about 100°C, allows us to enjoy water in all three common states of matter: solid, liquid, and gas. Earth has an atmosphere composed mostly of nitrogen with a significant percentage of oxygen, and small amounts of many other gases, including carbon dioxide and water vapor. Earth's dynamic atmosphere, water cycle, volcanism, and restless tectonic plates continually reconstruct the planet's surface, so the face of Earth is always fresh and changing. Consequently there is no record of the mighty bombardment that pelted the planet early in its history, and no rocks dating back to the time of the formation of Earth. And, of course, Earth has one moon, proportionally the largest moon in the Solar System. Earth is the one planet in the universe that we know to be home to the most amazing of all processes: life.

Mars

Fourth from the Sun is the red planet, Mars. Mars is small (about half the diameter of Earth) and arid, and has only the skimpiest of atmospheres, mostly carbon dioxide. It has two small moons, actually more like big rocks than nice spherical little planets, but they orbit Mars and qualify as moons.

Because the atmosphere is so thin and the planet, on balance, so cool (143°–17°C), liquid water does not exist on the surface. This was not always the case, however; there is ample evidence of monumental floods of water in the past. The floods and volcanism have erased much of the record of bombardment, but impact craters are evident over most of the planet's surface.

Mars has some of the most dramatic structures in the Solar System: the largest known volcanic mountain; a huge rift valley, many times larger than the Grand Canyon in Arizona; periodic dust storms that may engulf the entire planet; and polar caps of solid carbon dioxide that change size with the seasons.

The Martian day is just about exactly the same as ours here on Earth—just a tad longer. The year on Mars is 687 Earth days, not quite twice as long as the Earth year.

Asteroid Belt

Between the last rocky planet, Mars, and the first gas giant, Jupiter, is a region populated by thousands of rocky objects called **asteroids.** These range from almost 1000 km in diameter to 1 km. It is believed that these asteroids are material left over from the planet-forming era, and might have gotten together and formed a planet had there been a little more stuff in the region. As it is, they are destined to ride out the rest of the history of the Solar System as a batch of somewhat unpredictable pieces of matter.

Each asteroid is on its own particular orbit around the Sun, so no two are following the same path or traveling at exactly the same rate. For this reason, asteroids collide from time to time, which can change their direction. An asteroid on an unpredictable path could crash into something else...like a planet. Many scientists now think that such an object slammed into Earth some 65 million years ago, with catastrophic results.

Jupiter

The fifth planet, Jupiter, the first of the gas giants, is the heavyweight of the Solar System. It has a diameter of 143,000 km—11 times the diameter of Earth. In fact, if you remove the Sun from the picture, Jupiter has *half* of the remaining mass in the Solar System! (But that's still only 0.1%.) Jupiter has an atmosphere of hydrogen and helium, and may be thought of as all atmosphere and no planet at all. Because of the immense pressures deep in the core of Jupiter, however, the gases are compressed into a hot, liquidlike form of matter. Jupiter generates a lot of heat in its interior, accounting in part for the violent turbulence and storms that constantly sweep across its surface, including the Great Red Spot.

Jupiter does have moons—16 of them by current accounting, and a small ring, similar to Saturn's. Jupiter's moons provide some of the most interesting and provocative features of this awesome planet. Io is the most volcanically active location in the Solar System at this time. Europa is almost completely covered with water ice, and may have oceans of monumental proportions beneath the icy crust. Ganymede is the largest moon in the Solar System (larger even than planet Mercury), and is the first moon known to have its own magnetic field. Callisto is heavily cratered, suggesting a history similar to our own moon, but scientists are perplexed by the absence of smaller craters. Interestingly, all of Jupiter's largest moons keep one face toward their planet, just as the Moon always shows only one face to the Earth.

A day on Jupiter flies by, taking only 10 Earth hours. However, the Jovian year is long, equaling 11.86 Earth years. That's a lot of days in the year, but you could keep busy the whole time watching moons and trying to figure out how to calculate a month.

Saturn

The sixth planet, Saturn, is the true gas giant. Composed mostly of hydrogen and helium, its density is actually less than that of water. Can you imagine Saturn floating in a large tub of water?

Like Jupiter, Saturn is mostly atmosphere. It generates internal heat due to compression deep inside, and this heat may be at least partially responsible for the powerful storms surging across Saturn's surface. Like Jupiter, Saturn's most interesting attractions are in orbit around the planet.

First of all are the famous rings. Recent data from space probes shows that there are eight separate rings, like tracks around the planet. The origin and composition of the rings are still a matter of scientific investigation. Saturn also has multiple moons—18 confirmed at this time. Titan, the largest of the moons (just a bit larger than Mercury) generates the most scientific interest. Titan is surrounded by a dense nitrogen atmosphere. It has been suggested that this might be similar to the ancient atmosphere on Earth before life emerged.

Saturn's day is short, less than 11 Earth hours, but the year is really long, just about 30 Earth years.

Uranus and Neptune

Out in the cold reaches of the Solar System are Uranus (planet 7) and Neptune (planet 8), the other two gas giants, orbiting the Sun at 2.9 billion kilometers and 4.5 billion kilometers, respectively. Out there the energy from the Sun is so weak that it is of little use as a heat source. As a result, Uranus maintains a fairly constant –220°C, and the little-studied Neptune can't be any warmer.

Uranus boasts 15 moons, mostly frozen orbs of dirty ice, and Neptune has 8 moons. Triton, the largest moon of Neptune, is of interest to planetary scientists because of its colorful geological history. Triton displays active geysers that shoot nitrogen gas and dark dust several kilometers into the moon's thin atmosphere. And Triton's "reverse" orbit and high density suggest that it didn't form in orbit around Neptune, but was captured when it wandered by. Internal heating resulting from tidal surge may have melted the water on Triton, and it might have remained liquid for as long as a billion years. Scientists are curious to know more about this distant moon.

Again, these gas giants characteristically rotate rapidly, having days of 17 and 16 hours, respectively. And as you might expect, their years drag on forever. A year on Uranus is 84 Earth years, and on Neptune a startling 165 Earth years. Can you imagine how careful you would have to be in the future if you signed on to work at the Neptune science station for a year? Be *sure* to ask if that is an Earth year or a Neptune year.

Pluto

The ninth planet, Pluto, is a little tyke, not even as large as the Moon. There is no general agreement at this time as to where Pluto came from. It has been suggested that there might have been a host of similar objects on the perimeter of the Solar System, and Pluto is the only one that survived the early throes of Solar System formation.

Pluto follows an elliptical orbit, so at times it is the most distant planet from the Sun, and at other times it is closer to the Sun than Neptune is. Pluto is cold—so cold that when it is at its greatest distance from the Sun, its thin atmosphere freezes and falls to the planet's surface as a kind of snow.

Pluto has a moon, Charon, which orbits Pluto once every 6 Earth days. And Pluto rotates once every 6 Earth days. That means the day and the month are the same length on Pluto. But a year on Pluto takes 248 Earth years.

Comets

The only other significant players in the Solar System are the long-range wanderers, the comets. There are lots of these "dirty snowballs" that infrequently pass through the inner Solar System on exaggerated elliptical orbits. Most of the time they are way out in the far reaches of the Solar System, but they can create quite a lot of excitement when they drop in for a visit. The characteristic tail of a comet is a stream of tiny particles that flows off the comet body as it comes close to the Sun. When these minute particles are illuminated by the Sun, we can see one of nature's outstanding celestial light shows.

SPACE PROBES

For over 30 years NASA has been sending robotic probes into space, to go where no human has gone before. These robotic spacecraft act like extensions of ourselves, collecting information far out in the Solar System, and sending it back to Earth. Space probes have parts that mimic and extend human senses and abilities. Even if human astronauts can't visit other planets yet, robotic explorers can provide information that is the next best thing to being there. The table below compares humans and their robotic counterparts. But the table is not completely filled in. Can you think of the missing probe parts that function like our body parts?

Human body	Spacecraft counterpart
Body/torso	The housing that holds the spacecraft components and attaches to other devices. Also known as the "bus."
Neck	Scan platform. A part that pivots so that the instruments can point in the desired direction without reorienting the whole spacecraft.
Brain	
Nerves	
Skin	Blankets. For meteorite protection and temperature control—the spacecraft can't sweat so it uses radiators or louvers to get rid of excess heat.
Legs	Rocket motors. Space probes do not need to burn fuel constantly to move, only small rockets (thrusters) need fuel to change their orientation in space or to make course corrections. A small amount of fuel lasts many years.
Blood vessels	
Feet	
Arms	
Sense organs (eyes, nose, taste buds, touch sensors)	
Ears/voice	
Food/water	Batteries, fuel cells, solar panels for converting sunlight into electricity; radioisotope thermoelectric generators (RTGs) for converting heat from the decay of radioactive material into electricity—necessary in weak lighting far from the Sun.

NAVIGATION AND ORIENTATION

Imagine a spacecraft that has journeyed millions of miles through space for a first-ever flyby of a planet, and its cameras are pointed the wrong direction as it speeds past. Wouldn't that cause large-scale tearing of hair and gnashing of teeth back on Earth!

To help prevent such a disaster, spacecraft sight on the Sun and a bright star, such as Canopus, to help navigate and maintain orientation. If the probe is off course or pointing in the wrong direction, small rocket engines on the spacecraft can fire to make adjustments in the flight path and orientation.

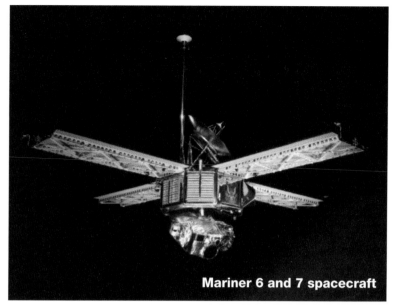

Mariner 6 and 7 spacecraft

Probes communicate with Earth using radio signals. The radio signal is weak if the probe is millions of kilometers from Earth. So NASA ground controllers use three huge "ears," steerable radio antennas (Deep Space Network) located in California, Australia, and Africa, to listen for the signal, which is then relayed to the probe's crew at a NASA mission-control center, such as Jet Propulsion Laboratory (JPL).

EXPLORING THE INNER SOLAR SYSTEM

From 1959 to 1972 NASA missions focused on exploration of the Moon and the inner Solar System—Mercury, Venus, and Mars. The first concentrated effort to get extraterrestrial information was directed at the Moon. In preparation for manned missions to the Moon, a series of **Ranger** spacecraft carried television cameras capable of transmitting close-up images of the lunar surface back to Earth.

Seven spacecraft in the **Mariner** program conducted the first surveys of the inner Solar System. Because they did not travel far from the Sun, all of the Mariners were powered by solar energy captured by either two or four solar panels covered with photovoltaic cells.

Mariner 2, the first Earth spacecraft to visit another planet, carried six instruments and a two-way radio to Venus in 1962. On the way to Venus, *Mariner 2* measured interplanetary dust,

magnetism, cosmic rays, and solar plasma. At Venus, *Mariner 2's* infrared and microwave instruments that could sense temperatures from afar found Venus's surface to be fire-hot—about 425°C. That's hotter than a pizza oven! Venus is heated, in part, by a strong greenhouse effect. Solar energy penetrates the thick carbon-dioxide atmosphere but cannot escape, so heat builds up. *Mariner 2* also discovered that Venus rotates from east to west, the opposite way from Earth.

In 1969 *Mariner 6* and *7* went to Mars. Instruments included two television cameras, an infrared radiometer (to measure surface temperature), and infrared and ultraviolet spectrometers, like specialized eyes, that analyzed wavelengths of light to determine atmosphere and surface chemical composition. The spacecraft approached to within 3550 km of the planet's surface (flyby) and transmitted almost 200 pictures of the planet Mars, Mars's moon Phobos, the northern and southern polar caps, and geological features, including volcanoes, huge impact craters, collapsed ridges, and craterless depressions. Analysis of the data revealed that the Mars polar caps are made of frozen carbon dioxide, or dry ice.

Mariner 9 was the first spacecraft to orbit another planet. Launched on May 30, 1971, the spacecraft circled Mars twice a day for a full year. It provided images of the surface and analyzed the atmosphere with infrared and ultraviolet instruments. The spacecraft gathered data on the atmosphere, density, pressure, and temperature, and information about the surface composition, temperature, and landforms.

When *Mariner 9* first arrived, Mars was almost totally obscured by dust storms, which lasted for a month. After the dust cleared, *Mariner 9* proceeded to reveal a planet very different from Earth—one with gigantic volcanoes and a grand canyon stretching 4800 km across its surface. More surprisingly, the relics of ancient riverbeds were carved in the landscape of this dry and dusty planet. *Mariner 9* surpassed all expectations by mapping 100% of the planet's surface and taking the first close-up images of the tiny Martian moons, Deimos and Phobos.

In 1975 NASA launched two new probes to Mars, **Viking 1** and **2.** Both probes were dual-purpose spacecraft, including an orbiter and a lander. Both took a little less than a year to travel to Mars (301 and 333 days). Everything worked admirably. The orbiters took thousands of high-resolution photos. The landers sent close-up images of the surface as well, but more important, they scooped up and analyzed the Martian soil for chemical composition and signs of life, "sniffed" and analyzed the atmosphere and weather, and placed seismometers to "feel" for Marsquakes. Viking provided a great stride forward in knowledge of the landforms, ancient water channels, and atmosphere on Mars, and confirmed what was suspected by scientists— the Martian soil was sterile, with no indication of life of any kind, past or present.

JOURNEY TO THE OUTER PLANETS

After the Apollo missions to the Moon in the late 1960s and early 1970s, NASA's interest shifted to the outer planets—Jupiter, Saturn, Uranus, and Neptune. Two spacecraft—the **Voyagers**—were sent. It took them up to 12 years to reach their remote destinations. Because the Sun's light becomes so faint in the outer Solar System, these spacecraft did not use solar power. Instead they operated with RTGs—radioisotopic thermoelectric generators. These devices, used on other deep-space missions, converted the heat produced by the radioactive decay of plutonium

Voyager spacecraft

into electricity to power instruments, computers, radios, and other systems.

The twin spacecraft, *Voyagers 1* and *2*, were launched in 1977. They were originally designed to conduct close-up studies of Jupiter and Saturn, Saturn's rings, and the larger moons of the two planets. The spacecraft were built to last 5 years, but, as the mission went on and achieved all of its original objectives, additional flybys of Uranus and Neptune became possible. NASA engineers on Earth reprogrammed the Voyagers to send them to new destinations. Their two-planet mission became a four-planet mission, and their 5 year lifetimes stretched to 12 years and more. They visited all the giant outer planets and observed their rings, magnetic fields, and their many moons, some for the first time.

The Voyagers took advantage of a rare geometric arrangement of the outer planets in the late 1970s and the 1980s, an arrangement that occurs only every 175 years or so. The unique positions of the planets allowed a spacecraft to whip past one planet, then the next, and the next, without needing large onboard propulsion systems. The flyby of each planet changed the spacecraft's direction and increased its speed enough to deliver it to the next destination. The technique is called **gravity assist.** Gravity attracts the probe, and as it swings around the planet, the probe "steals" rotational energy from the planet—its rotation actually slows a negligible amount, negligible because the planet has so much rotational energy. But the change to the speed of the probe is dramatic.

The gravity assist reduced the flight time to Neptune from 30 years to 12 years. *Voyager 1* reached Jupiter in 1979 and Saturn in 1980. *Voyager 2* visited Jupiter in 1979, Saturn in 1981, Uranus in 1986, and Neptune in 1989—an incredible four-planet tour.

Highlights of the Voyager missions included astonishingly detailed photos and other data on the planets of the outer Solar System (the gas giants), and their moons, magnetic fields, and rings. The amount of volcanism on Jupiter's satellite Io was the most unexpected discovery. Io turned out to be the most volcanically active body in the Solar System. Together, the Voyagers observed the eruption of nine volcanoes on Io. Plumes from the volcanoes extended to more than 300 km above the surface.

Jupiter's moon Europa displayed a large number of intersecting lines, which suggest a thin crust of water ice, maybe less than 30 km thick, possibly floating on a 50-km-deep ocean. This idea is being confirmed by even better images and data from the *Galileo*, which is now (1999) orbiting and imaging Jupiter and its moons.

Voyager found that Jupiter has a magnetic field that extends 3–7 million kilometers toward the Sun and stretches in a wind-sock shape at least as far as Saturn's orbit—a distance of 750 million kilometers. Images showed auroras (similar to Earth's northern lights) caused by ions falling along the magnetic field into the planet's atmosphere.

The Voyagers found more surprises and puzzles in Saturn's rings. Unexpected structures such as kinks and spokes were discovered, in addition to thin rings and broad, diffuse rings that couldn't be observed from Earth. Saturn's planet-size moon, Titan, was found to have a thick nitrogen-methane atmosphere. It is possible that complex hydrocarbons, the basic building blocks for life, coat the moon with a thick layer of organic matter. The chemistry in Titan's atmosphere may resemble the situation on Earth before life evolved.

Voyager 2 found ten new moons orbiting Uranus, bringing the total to 15. With its huge fault canyons as deep as 20 km, terraced layers, and a mixture of old and young surfaces, the moon Miranda is one of the strangest bodies yet seen in the Solar System. One theory suggests that Miranda is a recombination of material from an earlier time when the moon was broken to bits by a violent impact.

The strongest winds on any planet were measured on Neptune, blowing up to 2000 km/h. Neptune's moon Triton showed active geyserlike eruptions spewing nitrogen gas and dark dust several kilometers into the atmosphere.

The Vikings are now speeding away from the Sun, bound for deep space beyond the Solar System. Both carry a gold-plated disk that has recordings of music and sounds from Earth. The disk also includes images of Earth and a greeting message that describes where the probe came from.

Pioneer 10 and 11 spacecraft

MARS AND VENUS REVISITED

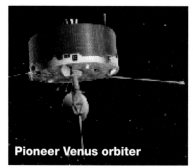
Pioneer Venus orbiter

Two drum-shaped **Pioneer** spacecraft visited Venus in 1978. The Pioneer Venus orbiter was equipped with a radar instrument that allowed it to "see" through the planet's dense cloud cover to study its surface features. The **Pioneer Venus multiprobe** carried four smaller probes that were dropped through the Venusian clouds.

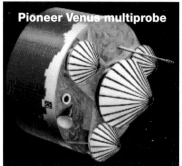
Pioneer Venus multiprobe

The probes radioed information about the planet's atmosphere during their descent toward the surface.

The *Magellan* space-craft was launched by the shuttle *Atlantis* in 1989. It looped around the Sun one-and-a-half times before arriving at Venus in 1990. It carried a sophisticated imaging radar device that mapped more than 98% of the planet's surface, discovering a host of intriguing features, including huge volcanic mounds and the longest lava channel ever seen. After finishing its radar mapping, *Magellan* also made global maps of Venus's gravity field. Flight controllers tested a

Magellan spacecraft

new maneuvering technique called **aerobraking.** Aerobraking uses a planet's atmosphere to slow or steer a spacecraft. The spacecraft finally plunged into the thick, hot Venusian atmosphere and was crushed by the pressure of Venus's atmosphere (90 times greater than Earth's atmospheric pressure).

The **Galileo** spacecraft has been in service for more than 10 years (launched October 18, 1989). After three gravity assists (Venus-Earth-Earth), *Galileo* passed through the asteroid belt and sped on to Jupiter, where it has been orbiting the planet since, investigating its atmosphere, satellites, and magnetosphere. During its duty at Jupiter, *Galileo* has passed close by volcanic moon Io; the Solar System's largest moon, Ganymede; and frozen moon Europa. The images from Europa show ice rafts on its surface, indicating an active, dynamic ocean under the frozen crust. There is likely more water on Europa than on Earth. And Europa has a thin oxygen atmosphere. *Galileo* also observed the thin rings around Jupiter, similar to the much larger rings around Saturn, and recorded huge thunderstorms (yes, water clouds) in the upper atmosphere of Jupiter itself.

In July 1994 *Galileo* was the only observer in position to witness the impact events when 20 fragments of comet Shoemaker-Levy 9 crashed into Jupiter on its dark side. These observations provided information about the energy released during such impacts.

BACK TO MARS

The **Mars Pathfinder** mission consisted of a stationary lander and a surface rover, the first of its kind. The mission had the primary objective of demonstrating the feasibility of low-cost landings on and exploration of the Martian surface. This two-part probe presented new challenges. The lander was the base station, and it stayed right where it happened to land. It had a powerful transmitter that communicated with Earth. The tiny rover crept around the Martian surface "looking at," "sniffing," and "poking at" interesting things it encountered. However, the rover's transmitter was very weak. It could communicate only with the lander. Messages from the control room in California to the rover had to be relayed through the base station in the lander. It worked, and the mission was a grand success.

Galileo spacecraft

Mars was once a water-rich planet, much more Earth-like than was anticipated. There was apparently a catastrophic flood between 1.8 and 3.5 billion years ago, and since that time Mars has been very un-Earth-like. The water has virtually disappeared, and the ancient floodplain hasn't changed since it formed.

The Pathfinder mission also added important information about the chemistry of the Martian rocks and soil and more refined data about the atmospheric conditions, including temperature fluctuations, pressure changes, and composition over time. Pathfinder's contributions to the advance of planetary science were in two areas: science and technology.

Sojourner

Another experiment was the landing technique. The spacecraft entered the Martian atmosphere directly, without going into orbit around the planet. The probe landed on Mars with the aid of parachutes, rockets, and airbags. It must have been a bit humorous to be on Mars that fine day in July 1997, and see a giant beach ball slam into the surface, bounce 16 times, and roll around for a while until it came to rest. In a while the balloons deflated, the walls of the pyramid flopped down, and out rolled a car the size of a toaster oven.

The rover, *Sojourner,* was a six-wheeled vehicle controlled by an Earth-based operator who used images obtained by both the rover and lander systems for navigation. The delay between the operator and *Mars Pathfinder* was 6 to 41 minutes, depending on the positions of Earth and Mars. So some independent control by the rover was necessary. *Sojourner* spent its first 10 days on Mars within 10 m of the lander. Extended trips away from the lander lasted about a month.

It is interesting to note how computer technology has changed over the history of NASA missions. During the 1960s the most powerful JPL computers had 16,000 bytes (16 kilobytes or 16K) of memory. Today most home computers have at least 24,000,000 bytes (24 megabytes or 24 MB) of memory. This phenomenal improvement in computer performance is just one technological factor that allows present missions and those planned for the future to be tremendously more sophisticated than those of 30 years ago.

THINK QUESTIONS

In what ways are robotic space probes similar to humans? Review the chart on the first page of this article and fill in the blanks with your ideas.

Venus and Mars are our closest neighboring planets. Like Earth they may have had water at one time. What evidence suggests water on these planets, and what might have happened to it?

If there is life elsewhere in the Solar System, where do you think it might be found? Why do you think so?

Mars Pathfinder landed on an ancient floodplain, covered with what appeared to be water-borne rocks, pebbles, and sands. It confirmed that

Mars Pathfinder stationary lander

PIONEER 10 PLAQUE

National Aeronautics and Space Administration

Pioneer 10, destined to be the first human-made object to travel beyond the Solar System, carries this plaque. It is designed to show scientifically educated inhabitants of some other star system, who might intercept it millions of years from now, when and where *Pioneer 10* was launched, and by what kind of beings. The design is engraved into a gold-anodized aluminum plate, 152 × 229 mm, attached to the spacecraft's antenna support struts, a position that will shield it to some degree from erosion by interstellar dust.

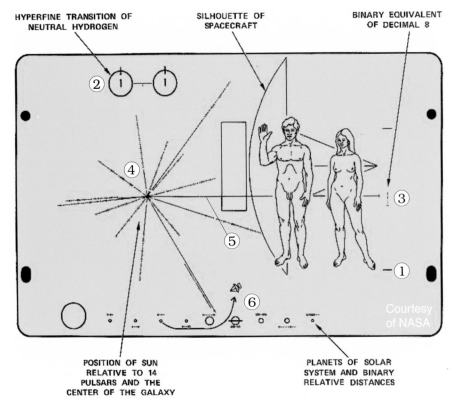

HYPERFINE TRANSITION OF NEUTRAL HYDROGEN

SILHOUETTE OF SPACECRAFT

BINARY EQUIVALENT OF DECIMAL 8

POSITION OF SUN RELATIVE TO 14 PULSARS AND THE CENTER OF THE GALAXY

PLANETS OF SOLAR SYSTEM AND BINARY RELATIVE DISTANCES

Courtesy of NASA

At the far right, the bracketing bars *(1)* show the height of the woman compared to the spacecraft. A figure *(2)* represents a reverse in the direction of spin of the electron in a hydrogen atom. This transition puts out a characteristic radio wave 21 cm long, so we are indicating that 21 cm is the standard unit of length used to interpret this plaque. The horizontal and vertical ticks *(3)* are a representation of the number 8 in binary form. Therefore, the woman is 8 × 21 cm = 168 cm tall. The human figures represent the type of creature that created *Pioneer 10*. The man's hand is raised in a gesture of goodwill.

The radial pattern *(4)* is perhaps the most important because it will tell *Pioneer 10's* finder where it came from and when it was launched.

The solid bars indicate distance, with the horizontal bar *(5)*, denoting the distance from the Sun to the center of our galaxy. The shorter solid bars represent directions and distances to various pulsars from our Sun, and the ticks following them are the periods of the pulsars in binary form. Pulsars are known to be slowing down, and if the rate of slowing is constant, an other-world scientist should be able to roughly deduce the time *Pioneer 10* was launched. Thus we have placed ourselves approximately in both space and time.

The drawing at the bottom *(6)* indicates the Solar System. The ticks accompanying each planet are the relative distance in binary form of that planet to the Sun. *Pioneer 10's* trajectory is shown as starting from the third planet, Earth.

Finding Planets outside the Solar System

Finding a planet circling a star other than our Sun is not easy. There are two problems. First, other stars are just too far away. A fairly close neighboring star might be only 33 light-years away. That is the distance light will travel in 33 years. And light travels fast! At 300,000 km/s light will travel 7.5 times around Earth in a second. In a year light will travel about ten trillion km (10,000,000,000,000 km). You can do the math to figure out how far light travels in 33 years. Looking for a planet the size of Earth around a star 33 light-years away would be like looking for a quarter 20 km away. Our most powerful telescope, the Hubble Space Telescope, could do the job except for problem number two.

Did you ever try to look for an airplane or bird flying in the sky in the direction of the Sun? You can't do it because the intense light from the Sun forces you to look away. Stars put out a tremendous amount of light. The glare from a star overpowers any other light in its vicinity. A planet, which produces no light of its own, would be impossible to see in the glare of its star.

Because of the tiny size of planets at such great distances, and the glare of the star, it is not possible to find planets by direct methods, that is, by looking for them. Planetary scientists, therefore, use indirect methods. They look for star wobble.

Current planet-hunting strategies rely on the fact that, as a planet orbits a star, not only does the star's gravity pull on the planet, but the planet's gravity pulls on the star as well. The first figure shows a planet orbiting a star.

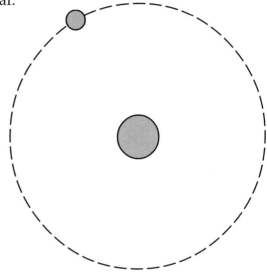

The next figure shows how, in reality, both the planet and the star circle around each other, around their common "center of gravity" or **barycenter.** Notice that the star is no longer the center around which the planet orbits; both star and planet orbit around the barycenter.

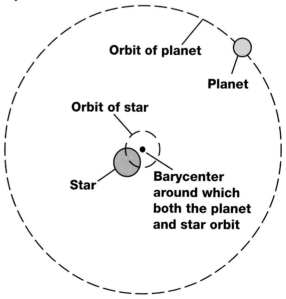

If the Solar System consisted of only the Sun and Jupiter, the barycenter would be just outside the Sun's visible surface.

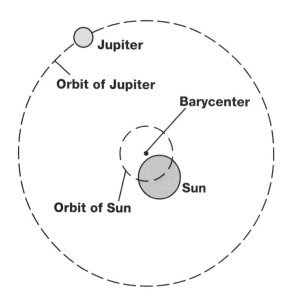

If our system had only the Sun and Earth (what a boring system), the barycenter would be deep within the Sun, but not at the center of the Sun.

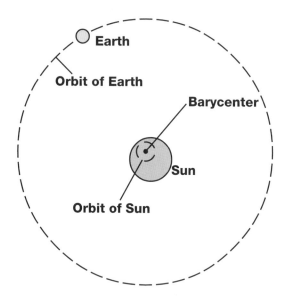

While attempts to view a planet directly have failed, *indirect* methods have given astronomers some evidence for the existence of other planets orbiting distant stars. Indirect strategies try to detect the movement of the star around which the planet orbits.

There are two indirect strategies that are being tried. The first, called **astrometry,** looks for back-and-forth movement of the star as it circles the barycenter of the system. The position of the star is observed and measured carefully for an extended period—a year as measured on the planet the scientists are searching for.

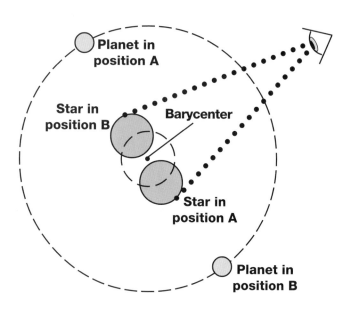

If there is a planet pulling on the star, the star should move, creating a perception that the star is wobbling back and forth. So far, not even the Hubble Space Telescope detected this back-and-forth wobble in any planetary system, but the idea is a good one.

98

The second method involves analyzing components of color in the star's light—its spectrum. This is **spectroscopic** planet-hunting.

Here's how spectroscopic planet-hunting works. Depending on what specific gases are in the star (e.g. helium, hydrogen, and others), certain wavelengths of light (specific colors of the rainbow) are given off. The exact wavelengths are very well defined. However, these wavelengths change slightly if the star is moving toward or away from the observer. The wavelength shifts toward blue if the star is moving toward us and toward red if the star is moving away from us. This is known as the **Doppler effect.**

The Doppler effect in light waves is similar to the effect you may have heard in sound waves as a siren or train horn passes by—the pitch of the sound changes dramatically from higher to lower. The pitch depends on whether the sound is coming toward you or going away from you. This happens because the sound waves get pushed together by the speed of the horn coming toward you, and stretched apart as the horn moves away from you. The greater the number of sound waves you hear in a unit of time, the higher the pitch of the sound.

Light is similar—the more light waves you see in a unit of time, the "bluer" the color will appear. Similarly, if light gets stretched out, fewer waves will arrive in a unit of time, and the color will shift toward red. If a star is in a small orbit around a barycenter, part of the time it will be coming toward an observer, and later it will be going away from the observer. The tiny shifts in color are what planet hunters look for.

In the fall of 1996, two Swiss astronomers rocked the world with their announcement that they had detected a Jupiter-mass object orbiting a nearby Sun-like star called 51 Pegasi. They used the spectroscopic technique to detect the planet. Since that time, a pair of astronomers, Geoffrey Marcy at San Francisco State University and Paul Butler at University of California, Berkeley, used spectroscopic techniques to discover at least eight more planet candidates. All these discoveries are being subjected to rigorous scrutiny and attempts at confirmation by the astronomical community.

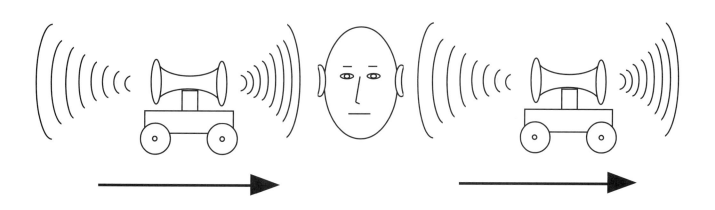

For centuries astronomers debated the probability of other planets being in the universe. Now we are on the verge of putting that debate to rest. But the discovery of planets elsewhere in the universe raises an even more interesting question: Is anything living on any of those planets?

The universe is a large playing field. Scientists looking for planets focus their attention on close stars—those within a few score light-years. In our Milky Way galaxy, however, there are perhaps 200,000,000 other stars distributed in a spinning disk that is about 100,000 light-years across and 10,000 light-years thick. The vast majority of the stars in our galaxy are too far away for searching at this time.

But it doesn't end there. The universe is populated with countless other galaxies, each with its assemblage of hundreds of millions of stars. Some of the galaxies are like ours in structure—a disk with starry arms reaching out from a central bulge—some are elliptical, and others have irregular shapes. And the distances between galaxies, even those in our local group, are so great that planet-hunting in these regions is out of the question at this time.

But knowing that planets do exist around other stars stimulates the imagination to dream of other worlds like Earth, maybe in our galaxy, and maybe beyond. And somewhere out there, at this very moment, there may be students in classrooms on those planets wondering...is there life anywhere else in the universe?

Think Question

Once we confirm other planetary systems, what do you think the next stage of exploration should be?

Spiral Galaxy M100, similar to the Milky Way

Spiral Galaxy NGC-4414

Overlapping elliptical and spiral galaxies

Spiral Galaxy NGC-4639

60 million light-years away

350 million light-years

78 million light-years

NAMING COMETS

Comet Hale-Bopp, Puckett Observatory, Mountain Town, GA

One way to become famous is to discover something and have it named after you.

In the field of astronomy, you can have a comet named for you if you discover it. Every night hundreds if not thousands of amateur astronomers are studying the sky, hoping to spot a new comet. If they locate one, they can submit their name and a description of the sighting to the Central Bureau for Astronomical Telegrams (CBAT).

This little-known bureau was founded in 1920 by the International Astronomical Union (IAU). It is subsidized by the Smithsonian Institution in Washington, DC. This bureau decides whether a person's name is assigned to a discovery in astronomy.

The CBAT is in a few crowded offices at Harvard University. When the bureau was created, notices of discoveries were sent by telegram, thus the bureau's name. Today, e-mail replaces telegrams.

A first sighting must be confirmed by other sky watchers. When it is confirmed, the bureau assigns a code describing the comet's location in the sky and when it was sighted. The name of the person who made the discovery is added in parentheses after the code. An average of two new discoveries are announced each year.

Naming a comet for yourself can become an obsession. Howard Brewington sold his home and electronics business in South Carolina and moved his family to a mountaintop in New Mexico just to search for new comets with his telescope. So far, he has found five.

The rules for getting your name attached to a discovery are unclear. Some people have their names associated with objects they did not discover. For example, most of the 900 comets discovered since 1920 are identified by the names of observatory directors who were not near a telescope when the comet was first sighted.

In 1994 the IAU began developing guidelines to standardize the rules for naming comets. Making guidelines appropriate and fair has not been easy. For example, what name would be assigned to a comet that five people in five locations discovered on the same night? Should all the names be listed? Or maybe draw one name out of the proverbial hat? Since 1939 there has been a three-name limit. When the IAU recently decided that two names would be enough, some Japanese astronomers became outraged. In Japan a comet was named Nishikawa-Takamizawa-Tago for the three people who discovered it at the same time.

Another problem is how to name a comet if you discover more than one. Currently five comets are named Levy. David Levy is a Vail, Arizona, astronomer who has been active in comet searching. To tell the comets apart, numbers are added to the discoverer's name—Levy 1, Levy 2, and so on.

But numbering comets presents still another problem. In the 1950s an astronomer named Harrington discovered two comets that were named Harrington 1 and Harrington 2. Then someone figured out that Harrington 1 was actually a rediscovery of comet Wolf 2. As a result comet Wolf 2 was renamed Wolf-Harrington. This caused Wolf 1 to be renamed comet Wolf, and comet Harrington 2 was changed to just comet Harrington. Confusing?

Some astronomers believe that assigning people's names to comets should be stopped. One argument for stopping the naming is that sometimes a discovery turns out to be embarrassing. Lubos Kahoutek discovered a comet in 1973, but when it swung close to Earth for everyone to see, it was a great disappointment—barely visible and definitely uninteresting to the general public. Now Kahoutek's name is associated with a "dud" comet.

Many astronomers would rather code the object in an accurate way. For instance, the 1995 discovery of comet Hale-Bopp (first observed at the same time but independently by Alan Hale and Tom Bopp) is coded C/ 1995 01. The code describes that the comet was discovered during the second half of July 1995 and that it will not return for more than 200 years.

The problem with using a code is that the code is very academic and is meaningless to the general public. A coded comet would make a news story seem less newsworthy. Instead of a headline reading "See comet Hale-Bopp tonight at 7:30 p.m.," it would read "See C/1995 01 tonight at 7:30 p.m." Coding loses the personal, human connection.

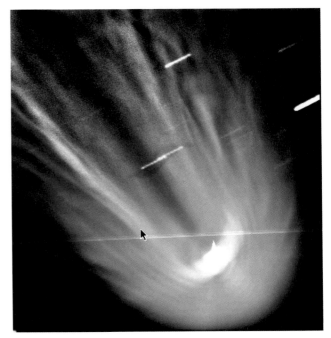

Comet Hale-Bopp, Tim Puckett, Puckett Observatory, Mountain Town, GA

Observer: David Lynch
Location: Puckett Observatory, Mountain Town, GA
Date: April 1, 1997, 01:50 UT

Two centuries ago, a comet was named after the person whose mathematical calculations accurately forecasted its return. English astronomer Edmond Halley was not alive to observe the comet that he correctly predicted would reappear in 1758—he died 16 years earlier. But his research and mathematical calculations were such that the comet was named Halley's comet.

By the end of the 19th century, only about 15 comets—the ones that return most frequently—officially carried the names of people. When CBAT came into being in 1920, it placed a greater emphasis on the discoverers' names. Then in 1931 the king of Denmark began offering gold medals to each person who first observed a new comet. From that time on, competition to be the first to see a comet was under way.

Clearly the IAU has not resolved the problem of how to properly and fairly name comets. Reread the information above and list the issues that must be considered as well as the arguments for and against each resolution that has been tried. If you come up with a solution that you think is worthy of consideration, write a letter to the IAU that describes a way to name comets that will please both the astronomers and the general public.

International Astronomy Union
Mail Stop 18
Smithsonian Astrophysical Observatory
60 Garden Street
Cambridge, MA 02138
U.S.A.